A GUIDE
FOR
SOFTWARE ENTREPRENEURS

A GUIDE
FOR
SOFTWARE ENTREPRENEURS

A. L. FRANK

PRENTICE-HALL, INC., Englewood Cliffs, New Jersey 07632

Library of Congress Cataloging in Publication Data

Frank, A. L.
  A guide for software entrepreneurs.

  Includes bibliographical references and index.
  1. Computer service industry—Management.   I. Title.
HD9696.C62F6   001.64′25′068   82-5348
ISBN 0-13-370726-1   AACR2

Editorial/production supervision by Linda Mihatov Paskiet
Cover design by Edsal Enterprises
Manufacturing buyer: Gordon Osbourne

Printed in the United States of America

10 9 8 7 6 5 4 3 2 1

ISBN 0-13-370726-1

PRENTICE-HALL INTERNATIONAL, INC., *London*
PRENTICE-HALL OF AUSTRALIA PTY. LIMITED, *Sydney*
PRENTICE-HALL CANADA, INC., *Toronto*
PRENTICE-HALL OF INDIA PRIVATE LIMITED, *New Delhi*
PRENTICE-HALL OF JAPAN, INC., *Tokyo*
PRENTICE-HALL OF SOUTHEAST ASIA PTE. LTD., *Singapore*
WHITEHALL BOOKS LIMITED, *Wellington, New Zealand*

To the memories
of my mother and father,
Bertha and David Frank,
and to the caring and kindness
of my wife,
Barbara M. Lippe

CONTENTS

PREFACE

Probably no group in the history of industrialized society has been more uniquely suited for entrepreneurship than computer programmers. There are many factors that are responsible for this phenomenon.

First of all, the demand for programmers and programs has far exceeded the supply. The shortage has led to an increased ease of programmer mobility—an indicator associated with many entrepreneurial ventures. After all, if one is easily able to obtain a job, then the risk of an entrepreneurial venture is minimized. With the experts predicting even more shortages, there will be increased entrepreneurial activities.

Second, there is a creative trend associated with the better programmers. Anyone who has tried to tell a programmer how to program, let alone what to program, recognizes the rebellious nature of the creative programmer. A good system design will satisfy user needs. However, the exact implementation of a system is up to the programmer. This creative ownership of the end product is a very encouraging sign that new and better software systems will be developed. Any factor that accounts for creativity will also be found to cause increased entrepreneurial activities.

Third, there is no dominant independent (i.e., nonhardware manufacturer) software vendor. When no one firm has totally captured the market, new entries have a higher probability of success. Thus programmers can and do develop software packages that can be sold to significant numbers of clients. There are some trends that indicate major consolidations are in store for the software industry. However, increased merger and acquisition activities encourage would-be entrepreneurs to enter the market.

With these positive factors, one might question the need for a guide to software entrepreneurship. However, the fact is that most computer professionals who desire to become entrepreneurs never get started. There has been little offered in the way of academic computer science courses to provide basic business skills for programmers. Company training programs have obviously avoided instructing would-be entrepreneurs how to break away from the company. The general entrepreneurial literature is extensive and rich, but it usually does not deal directly with the very unique aspects of computer software.

In some ways the software entrepreneur is like the money-motivated artist. Unfortunately for the artist, the business community has been slow to develop a widely accessible pathway for entrepreneurial success. Fortunately for the software developer, the basic mode of launching a business is supported by the industry structure.

This book takes a very structured and yet informal approach to providing some basic rules for the software entrepreneur. By following the course of an entrepreneurial venture, we will reinforce these rules.

The rules and examples in the book are based on the personal experience of numerous software entrepreneurs. Most examples are composites of their activity. Whenever possible the orientation is to the general software marketplace. That target includes all sizes and uses of software. However, because the personal computing market is in the formative stage, fewer hard facts are available. Yet microcomputer specialists should not be discouraged. By using some of the same principles that have been successful with larger software ventures, the micro specialist can be far better prepared than the competition.

Additionally, it is important to note that this book is business oriented rather than technically oriented. The emphasis is on planning and marketing with a large portion of the text devoted to showing how to bring out and sell a product profitably. Only brief mention is made of some very good existing technical skills for developing and maintaining software. There are excellent references available in this latter area. Most software ventures succeed or fail for purely business reasons. Some very poor technical products with totally inelegant code have led to major successes while many very good technical creations have failed miserably.

First we stress the business aspect of the software area by reviewing what a software entrepreneurial venture is and then following through with business planning and formation activities. We then examine product planning and product design, implementation, and testing. The next step in the life of a software firm deals with marketing and sales planning, the sales process, and sales management. We then discuss support and follow-on business. We conclude by an examination of the rewards from an entrepreneurial venture.

There are several supplemental appendices. One deals with venture capital and business planning; another provides materials related to software legal protection; still another is devoted to some business fundamentals; another supplies a detailed guideline for seminar preparation; finally, there is a recount of the view of a very large software firm toward the software entrepreneur.

At this point we need to issue a plea for some common sense courtesy and morality. Just because one intends to embark on an entrepreneurial venture, one does not have to abandon friends. In fact, extra courtesy and kindness might be required to get others to put up with the exceptional strains and time demands associated with a new venture. Some of the better associations in the software industry are based on friendships and some of the most respected businesspeople still take the time to thank a receptionist after a meeting. Along with courtesy is the true concept of morality, not necessarily from a religious standpoint but from an ethical sense. It is not necessary that someone else should suffer in order for the entrepreneur to benefit. Past employers, competitors, and vendors may make attractive targets for rip-offs that are within the law. However, remember that one major intangible asset of a new venture is the founder's reputation. A lot of new ventures are begun *after* terminating employment and *after* contracting for computer time and *after* being certain not to steal another's ideas. In the long run, honesty is a very important attribute.

The road to success as a software entrepreneur is not an impossible one. As with any new activity, there are some risks and some rewards. The theme of this book is minimizing the risks and maximizing the rewards. There are no guarantees for success, yet every day small computer software firms make large deposits in bank accounts. It is hoped that this book will help you to join their ranks. Good luck!

A. L. Frank

A GUIDE
FOR
SOFTWARE ENTREPRENEURS

Chapter 1

INTRODUCTION
What Is a Software Entrepreneur?

1.1 THE FUNDAMENTAL RULE

An entrepreneur is "a person who organizes and manages a business enterprise, assuming the risk for the sake of profit" (*Webster's New World Dictionary,* The World Publishing Co., 1970). This book is designed to provide special benefits to software entrepreneurs, those unique individuals who develop usable programs and take the initiative to enter the software industry assuming risk for the sake of profits.

Like any effort, entrepreneurship requires that certain guidelines be followed. Careful adherence to these rules will increase the likelihood of success. The following journey through the life of an entrepreneurial venture will provide many practical suggestions. *The* fundamental rule of software entrepreneurship is:

ALL EFFORTS IN A SOFTWARE BUSINESS SHOULD BE DIRECTED AT GENERATING A PROFIT.

To many this rule may seem obvious. However, as we examine the steps in an entrepreneurial venture, we will continue to describe ways to enforce the fundamental principle. As we will see, almost any software business can be managed in such a way as to generate a profit. With a little skill and careful adherence to the fundamental rule, a would-be entrepreneur can achieve positive results. Of course, profit is a multifaceted word. We will spend considerable time examining profit. For the time being we will assume that profit is the monetary reward from a business venture. Profit translates

1

into the ability to have money to spend, to save, to invest, or to do with whatever your heart desires.

1.2 THE ENTREPRENEURIAL FACTORS

Before examining some successful entrepreneurial ventures, we should point out that there are several stages of potential entry into a software venture. You may already have a product developed or you may be thinking of a product. It's worthwhile to ask yourself what you have developed and who would care. If you can answer these two questions, you can begin to put the venture in proper perspective.

There are many successful software entrepreneurial ventures. In order better to understand some of the basic ingredients that can make your effort successful, we will look at the factors that lead to these successes. The definition of an entrepreneur guides our study of these ventures.

First of all, successful entrepreneurs *organize* their business undertakings. They spend a great deal of time and energy planning how to set up their businesses. There are many reasons for this preparation. The business must adhere to legal requirements such as professional licenses. The venture must consider various marketing factors such as naming of products. The enterprise must take advantage of tax and liability regulations. Just as important, the effort must satisfy personal ego considerations such as establishing one's own company. The major reason that entrepreneurs spend time, money, and effort organizing their business is to generate profits. In a later chapter we will examine these organizational requirements and see how they can affect a firm's profits. It is not surprising that most successful entrepreneurs have recognized this important factor and, years after they initiate their activity, they can recall the reasons for choosing its structure.

Second, successful entrepreneurs *manage* their businesses. There are numerous management styles and techniques, ranging from a dictatorial "Do it or else. . ." to a Socratic "What do you think about. . .?" There are two very important aspects of management style. The first is that almost all management formats are successful if certain basic techniques are utilized. The fact that you are a humanist and do not wish to offend your fellow workers does not mean that you cannot be a successful manager. You do not have to change your basic style. Successful entrepreneurs learn to use their comfort with and belief in themselves to instill respect from others. That respect translates into very powerful leadership skills. The second is that you will likely spend as much time managing yourself as you do others, and by using the same techniques. Again, the only reason to spend time managing is to generate a profit. For example, if a manager recognizes that profit is related to programmer productivity and there is little leverage in telling a programmer how to write each line of code, the successful manager stays away from such detailed involvement. By managing your efforts to maximize profits you can create a successful enterprise. Remember you can develop and learn management skills to direct your business enterprise to generate a profit. We'll look at many of these skills, but if you emphasize comfort and self-management you'll have a head start.

Third, successful entrepreneurs recognize that what they are doing is a *business undertaking*. Your business can be your hobby, your love, or your therapy, but above all it is a business. Thus, successful entrepreneurs may have a great deal of fun in their adventure, but they run a business in order to generate a profit. If you think the emphasis on the profit motivation is repetitive, keep in mind that this emphasis is essential.

Fourth, successful entrepreneurs *assume a risk*. This book will impart procedures to reduce the risk, but remember that risk is an inherent part of software entrepreneurship. What separates the dreamer from the success is that while the former may be aware of the potential reward, the latter is willing to take a chance to gain it. The somewhat glorified picture of a calm, cool, and brave executive examining probabilistic risk models, making a decision, and then calmly reaping the rewards of the decision is absurd. The successful entrepreneur suffers some fear of failure but accepts this as part of the effort. If you are not aware of this fear, you are either in an altered state of consciousness or you are closing your mind to reality. The successful entrepreneur takes risks, not to be a hero or a masochist, but rather because he or she can see the potential profit associated with that risk.

Considering the above four factors (organization, management, business undertaking, and risk assumption), now let's reexamine the fundamental rule to see how it can be justified.

Everyone has individual desires. Some people enjoy material items, such as expensive foreign cars, airplanes, rare wines, beautiful clothes. Others have desires to travel—a weekend dining in Paris or climbing a Yosemite peak. A few thrive on seeing their name (or something with personal identity) in print. Some relish the fact that 25,000 passengers per day may be serviced by "their" module in a reservation system. Many individuals thrive on work, enjoy creating things, solving problems, and accomplishing goals. These are all worthwhile pursuits, and none is usually available without money. If you are unwilling to admit that the things you enjoy are available with greater ease and comfort with money, then you should probably trade in this book at your earliest convenience.

1.3 TYPES OF ENTREPRENEURS

By now you should have noticed that we continue to get back to the concept of profit or monetary reward. You may be very happy without monetary rewards. Perhaps you prefer to help someone else achieve great financial success while you earn a very comfortable living. However, if you limit yourself to that role, you will not be a successful entrepreneur.

This book is for the entrepreneur. To a great extent, the name of the game in entrepreneurship is to minimize lost energy. If you stop reading this book now and remember to evolve only those decision-making strategies that are based on the simple rule that *all efforts in a software business should be directed at generating a profit,* you have greatly increased your chance of success.

There are basically two types of entrepreneurs. One is interested in starting a venture as a vehicle for making money and will likely sell out after achieving a set of goals. The second wishes to build a company that will be a lasting entity. For both, the primary goal is to generate a profit. However, the secondary reasons for the effort differ.

There are also many types of individuals in the software field who make valuable contributions but are not entrepreneurs. In fact, many are more hobbyists than professionals. With the advent of easy-to-use, inexpensive microcomputer technology, there is truly a form of recreational software development. There are also many hobbyists joining with professional programmers to establish today's pipeline of entrepreneurial ventures. Currently there are several adolescent programmer/hobbyists who have software royalty contracts worth hundreds of thousands of dollars. These programmer/hobbyists have, by entering the business world, become entrepreneurs. Many of these semiprofessional programmers live quite well as a result of their programs. Additionally, professional programmers develop programs during the course of their work which generate substantial bonuses and fees. Both the teenage authors and the professional programmers enjoy the benefits of their efforts because they crossed the entrepreneurial line. They said, "I want to start a business," and from that point on, their motivation was a conscious one of generating profit.

We have spent quite a bit of time talking about the profit motivation. We will now follow the path of the successful entrepreneur through the many steps of a business, beginning with how to begin the enterprise.

--------------------- **REVIEW** ---------------------

1. Most would-be entrepreneurs have an activity in mind. What is yours? What packages do you have in mind? What is the potential market? Write out a definition of it and use it throughout this book.

2. Begin right now with the concept of organization. Take your definition and begin to think how you wish to organize it. Do you want others involved? How soon will you need to associate with programmers, salespeople, and others?

3. Have you ever managed people? If so, what is your style? Think about how you will manage the following:
   (a) Your secretary refuses to work late in order to get out a proposal.
   (b) A programmer on your staff works very hard but continues to miss deadlines.
   (c) You have a salesperson who always brings in the business yet continues to complain that your product misses some basic points.
   (d) You have a star programmer who is tried of coding and wants a new challenge and yet your star is doing an important job.

4. How does a business enterprise differ from a hobby? A project? Your job?

5. List the risks of starting your business. Then list your reactions to these.

6. Why do you want to start a business?

7. List your goals from a monetary standpoint. What is the least you can earn over the next three years? What would you like to earn?

8. If your business is successful, what will you do next?

This book will help you answer these questions.

REFERENCES

There are numerous entrepreneurial publications, too many even to begin a recommended list. As a special project, go to your library and look at the business periodicals that have articles on new companies. Choose two or three publications and read back issues. Each month find an additional publication. Begin to build your own reference library and filing system. If you don't already, start to read the business section of your local newspaper. Certainly read *The Wall Street Journal*. Most successful entrepreneurs spend four to eight hours per week reading, a major part of that time being devoted to business publications. Of course, you should retain copies of any articles that are of interest. The remaining chapters of this book list sample references. In addition, the business section of any public library holds dozens of books dealing with the subjects. A good idea is to visit your local book store and try to obtain at least one book for each area of concern. Remember, the references are merely to help you get started in the area of outside reading; they are not intended to be either an exclusive or complete list of publications.

Chapter 2

FORMATION
How to Begin a Business

2.1 *THE T-CHART PLANNING PROCESS*

Quite often guides to business formation suggest that the entrepreneur first contact an attorney in order to form a company. As we will see in the next chapter, the type of business entity, whether sole proprietorship, partnership, or corporation, should be a function of some very basic business objectives. To maximize profits, we need to know how to make a proper choice of business form. In fact, a good attorney will ask questions that can be answered only after the business objectives are defined.

Objectives are very valuable input to the total business process. One requirement for organizing a successful business is the creation of a set of working papers which can be reviewed and revised. The software entrepreneur should retain all working documents. The method may vary with individual requirements and styles. For some, a bound journal is best. Others may prefer a three-ring loose-leaf notebook. Still others may set up a filing system. Take your choice, but stick with it. These documents are being prepared to maximize profit. They will be referred to frequently. Sometimes it will be appropriate to retrieve older papers. Retention *and* access are key to survival. Decide now what system you are going to use and begin using it by organizing your notes from this book.

One good way to begin to define a business is to draw a T-chart. On the left-hand side of the "T" write the words "Goals and Objectives," and on the right-hand side write "How." By now we will assume you agree that the primary goal is to maximize profit. Thus, this chart is titled "Maximize Profit." (See Figure 2.1.)

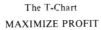

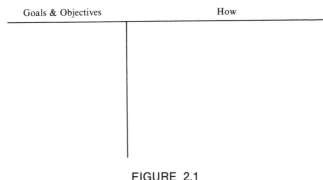

FIGURE 2.1

2.2 CASE STUDIES

In order to study this planning process, we will examine three potential business activities.

In Case A, John Jones is a systems programmer working for a large aerospace corporation. He has gotten tired of the inefficiencies he sees in the standard IBM copy utility and has rewritten it. Several of his friends of the local MVS (an IBM operating system) users' group have asked him for his program. One night, after working until 5 A.M. trying to get stand-alone time to solve an undocumented operating system problem, John decides he would like to sell his program and retire from the strange time demands he faces as a systems programmer.

In Case B, Judy Smith is an analyst for a large bank and is also a project leader for a new personnel system. Judy has designed two other personnel systems and is now acutely aware that there is some commonality in these applications. She intuitively believes that other companies would purchase a well-designed system. She wants to design and build a generalized system to sell.

In Case C, Joe Brown is a mechanical engineer. Although not trained as a programmer, Joe has recently purchased a home computer and, much to his delight, has determined that he can program a set of basic structural analysis programs that he uses almost daily in his job. Joe believes that other engineers have similar needs and he can sell them a total turnkey system including the hardware (the home computer) and software (his applications).

Before examining each of these cases, let's look at a few fundamentals of business ethics, and perhaps law. Short of a very strong and enforceable employment agreement there is little to prevent John, Judy, and Joe from legally working on their efforts at night while employed. Of course, there is a strong legal requirement that they do not use any resources or any trade secrets of the company. However, the better view is that an entrepreneur will make the break prior to beginning. We'll discuss the legal aspects

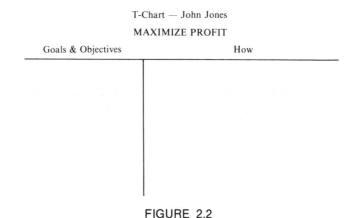

T-Chart — John Jones
MAXIMIZE PROFIT

Goals & Objectives	How

FIGURE 2.2

of this later. Most industry professionals shy away from entrepreneurial ventures that may be tainted because of conflicts of interest.

Let's begin with Case A. John Jones has read the first chapter of this book and he recognizes that above all he wishes to maximize profit. He prepares his Goals and Objectives as in Figure 2.2. John believes that he can sell his program to other system programmers and that he must build a new copy utility to be called JJCOPY. He then enters this as a goal (Figure 2.3). In order to be certain JJCOPY is great, John knows he must obtain performance results as well as be certain that it is error-free. To do this he must add two more goals: "Performance test" and "User test" (Figure 2.4). As much as he dislikes the thought, John knows that documentation is required. Thus "Document JJCOPY" is added to the chart, as in Figure 2.5. Finally, John wants to sell the system and so "Sell JJCOPY" is included (Figure 2.6). Now John can create a rough plan. He isn't going to create a 50-page strategic planning document, but rather simply begin to determine how to achieve each of his objectives.

Goal number 1 is to build JJCOPY. How does he plan to do this? First of all he

T-Chart — John Jones
MAXIMIZE PROFIT

Goals & Objectives	How
1. Build JJCOPY	

FIGURE 2.3

T-Chart — John Jones

MAXIMIZE PROFIT

Goals & Objectives	How
1. Build JJCOPY 2. Performance test 3. User test	

FIGURE 2.4

T-Chart — John Jones

MAXIMIZE PROFIT

Goals & Objectives	How
1. Build JJCOPY 2. Performance test 3. User test 4. Document JJCOPY	

FIGURE 2.5

T-Chart — John Jones

MAXIMIZE PROFIT

Goals & Objectives	How
1. Build JJCOPY 2. Performance test 3. User test 4. Document JJCOPY 5. Sell JJCOPY	

FIGURE 2.6

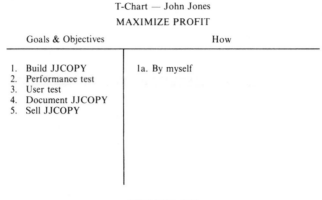

FIGURE 2.7

believes he can do this project alone. This becomes his first "How," listed as 1.a, as shown in Figure 2.7. Now John has some of the design completed, but he has a few new ideas. He must complete the design and then write the code, and he adds these as shown in Figure 2.8. (Note as a warning of things to come, John should not be using his current employer's computer and also should not violate any employment agreements.) Before performance testing John wants to test the system to check for errors and tune the code, and he makes this 1.d (Figure 2.9). The second goal, performance testing, is simple for John. He will create several job streams and will measure CPU resources used, with standard available tools. These become 2.a and 2.b, as in Figure 2.10. User testing, goal number 3, is a little more difficult. After some careful thought, he determines that he can find several friends to install the system and report the results. He adds these as shown in Figure 2.11. John not only hates to document, but he also recognizes that he is a poor writer. Thus he believes he should find outside help. He is friendly with several of his company's documentation group and he wants to hire one of them as a part-time employee to prepare the documentation. Thus, for goal number

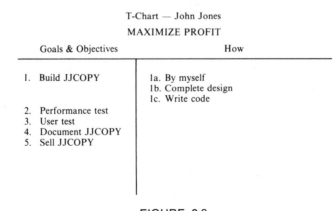

FIGURE 2.8

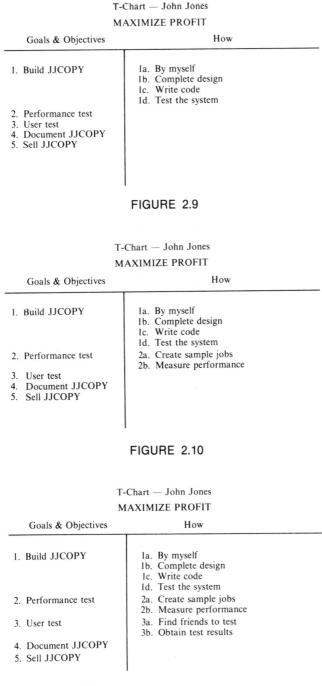

T-Chart — John Jones

MAXIMIZE PROFIT

Goals & Objectives	How
1. Build JJCOPY	1a. By myself 1b. Complete design 1c. Write code 1d. Test the system
2. Performance test 3. User test 4. Document JJCOPY 5. Sell JJCOPY	

FIGURE 2.9

T-Chart — John Jones

MAXIMIZE PROFIT

Goals & Objectives	How
1. Build JJCOPY	1a. By myself 1b. Complete design 1c. Write code 1d. Test the system
2. Performance test	2a. Create sample jobs 2b. Measure performance
3. User test 4. Document JJCOPY 5. Sell JJCOPY	

FIGURE 2.10

T-Chart — John Jones

MAXIMIZE PROFIT

Goals & Objectives	How
1. Build JJCOPY	1a. By myself 1b. Complete design 1c. Write code 1d. Test the system
2. Performance test	2a. Create sample jobs 2b. Measure performance
3. User test	3a. Find friends to test 3b. Obtain test results
4. Document JJCOPY 5. Sell JJCOPY	

FIGURE 2.11

T-Chart — John Jones

MAXIMIZE PROFIT

Goals & Objectives	How
1. Build JJCOPY	1a. By myself
	1b. Complete design
	1c. Write code
	1d. Test the system
2. Performance test	2a. Create sample jobs
	2b. Measure performance
3. User test	3a. Find friends to test
	3b. Obtain test results
4. Document JJCOPY	4a. Hire parttime documentation analyst
5. Sell JJCOPY	

FIGURE 2.12

4, "Hire part-time documentation analyst" is added (Figure 2.12). John dislikes salespeople and he believes that he can sell JJCOPY to at least fifteen local installations by announcing it at his local MVS user group. Thus 5.a, "Announce at MVS user group," is included, as in Figure 2.13.

If these planning techniques seem simple, they are. Even with these unsophisticated methods, John has made some very basic and fundamental decisions. First of all, he will work alone except for hiring a documentation writer. Second, he is going to get friends to test his system. Third, he knows he must set up a performance test. Finally, he has to be prepared to present the system to his local users group. The T-chart developed is a rough plan and will be very useful to John as he discusses his plans with others and directs his business effort.

This planning process is free form and individual-oriented, yet it is basic and does not require extensive training. We will carry out the same procedure for Case B and Case C to see how they differ.

T-Chart — John Jones

MAXIMIZE PROFIT

Goals & Objectives	How
1. Build JJCOPY	1a. By myself
	1b. Complete design
	1c. Write code
	1d. Test the system
2. Performance test	2a. Create sample jobs
	2b. Measure performance
3. User test	3a. Find friends to test
	3b. Obtain test results
4. Document JJCOPY	4a. Hire parttime documentation analyst
5. Sell JJCOPY	5a. Announce at MVS user group

FIGURE 2.13

T-Chart — Judy Smith

MAXIMIZE PROFIT

Goals & Objectives	How
1. Study personnel systems 2. Design a generalized, online system 3. Program the system under IMS 4. Document the system 5. Test the system 6. Sell the system 7. Enhance the system for CICS	

FIGURE 2.14

In Case B, Judy determines that her Goals and Objectives are as shown in Figure 2.14.

Judy has decided that she needs to study existing personnel systems and that when she designs the system, it will be for terminal systems under IMS (an IBM proprietary teleprocessing-data base system). She also knows she must document and test the system. Obviously, she hopes to sell the package to large companies with IMS installed on their computer system. Finally, she wishes to enhance the system for CICS operation.

Judy then determines how she will accomplish these goals and objectives. Her plan is shown in Figure 2.15.

T-Chart — Judy Smith

MAXIMIZE PROFIT

Goals & Objectives	How
1. Study personnel systems	1a. Attend AMA seminar 1b. Visit local sites
2. Design a generalized, online system	2a. Develop screen formats 2b. Lay out data structures 2c. Define transactions
3. Program the system under IMS	3a. Hire IMS programmers 3b. Find IMS development time
4. Document the system	4a. Use a project notebook 4b. Obtain hard copies of the screens 4c. Develop a menu
5. Test the system	5a. Create a test plan 5b. Maintain a test log
6. Sell the system	6a. Hire a parttime salesperson
7. Enhance the system for CICS	7a. Redesign program and test

FIGURE 2.15

Judy is prepared to start work. She wants to research personnel systems. She has chosen to leave her present job and to personally design the system, but wants to use contract programmers and an outside computer service. She will use her normal existing methods to design the system. She will test the system herself with help from the hired programmers. She plans to employ a part-time salesperson. Finally, she will redesign the system for CICS and follow the above procedures for her effort. Note the differences between Judy's and John's goals, as well as the differences in their "How's." Both of them can achieve their goals equally well.

In Case C, Joe begins to prepare his structural design turnkey system by detailing his efforts as in Figure 2.16.

Joe already knows how his system should perform. He will take a set of standard algorithms and program these in the BASIC programming language. He must compare his developed system with his work system to be certain of accuracy and performance. Joe wishes to announce his product at the annual Structural Engineer's convention and to write a paper describing the system for his society's journal. He will sell the final product to the members of this society. Finally, Joe will sell the system locally. He plans to accomplish these goals by the means listed in Figure 2.17.

Joe already knows how to begin his business. First of all he will not redo the basic algorithm designs but will pick and choose what he wants from the existing published literature. He will program the system himself and compare the results to his system at work. These results all serve as the basis for the paper he wishes to write. He wants to sell the hardware by showing off his system at a trade show and using a local storeroom from which to show and distribute his system.

Have John, Judy, and Joe forgotten important items? Probably. But that's the whole point of this process. They can each review their T-charts and add elements. Obviously, they should question each item as to whether it generates profit. If not, the entrepreneur must closely examine the item and consider removing it. This whole process is simple and will take a few hours at most. However, once produced, it becomes a rough plan which can be used to define requirements.

T-Chart — Joe Brown

MAXIMIZE PROFIT

Goals & Objectives	How
1. Design a set of algorithms 2. Program a system in BASIC 3. Test system usability 4. Become an OEM hardware vendor 5. Obtain general industry visibility 6. Establish a professional image 7. Sell the system locally	

FIGURE 2.16

T-Chart — Joe Brown

MAXIMIZE PROFIT

Goals & Objectives	How
1. Design a set of algorithms	1a. Use textbook equations
	1b. Eliminate infrequently used calculations
2. Program a system in BASIC	2a. Program during evenings and weekends
3. Test system usability	3a. Develop test cases
	3b. Compare results
	3c. Document test
4. Become an OEM hardware vendor	4a. Talk to company purchasing agents for ideas
	4b. Discuss with local computer stores
5. Obtain general industry visibility	5a. Reserve space a structural engineering convention
	5b. Hire commercial artist to design booth
6. Establish a professional image	6a. Use test results to publish a paper
	6b. Have a technical writer review the materials
7. Sell the system locally	7a. Get showroom
	7b. Hire clerk

FIGURE 2.17

2.3 RESOURCES

Requirements can be viewed as resources. The budding software entrepreneur does not have unlimited resources, so it is exceptionally important at this stage realistically to define the required resources and then to determine if they are available. Unfortunately, many beginning entrepreneurs, swept up in enthusiasm, fail to perform this simple exercise. Thus they make a false start without sufficient financial or other resources to carry the activity through to its first logical plateau. Fortunately, proper techniques allow the entrepreneur to recover the effort, but not without much unnecessary suffering.

There are three types of resources: technical, informational, and monetary.

Technical resources include skills required for such functions as documentation, data-base knowledge, systems programming, and marketing. Businesses also require access to certain technologies in order to complete a project, such as certain computer specifications, programming tools, or specialized error-solving skills.

The information resources required by a software entrepreneurial venture include market research data such as market size, financial techniques such as OEM discounts, and business practices such as financial management.

There are two basic types of monetary resources necessary for a new company: the cost of doing business and the cost of living. The money required to do business consists of operating expenses such as office, supplies, telephones, computer expenses, salaries, and professional fees. These will be detailed in a section on budgeting in a later chapter. For now we can sit down with our T-chart and estimate costs. The cost of living is the entrepreneur's required incremental outflow to survive during the business enterprise. If you plan to continue to work full-time, this cost may be negligible. If you plan to abandon your job, you should sit down and develop a bare bones household budget.

For each "How" on the T-chart, the software entrepreneur should now list resources. Examining Case A, we can see what John would list as the resources required for the JJCOPY system.

1. Public domain descriptions of the IBM utility.
2. Computer facilities on which to code. (John chooses the computer at work *after* obtaining written permission from his current employer.)
3. A set of sample jobs using JJCOPY.
4. A performance measuring tool which he borrows with permission of a software vendor.
5. An agreement with the companies of friends to test JJCOPY.
6. Money agreement.
7. A documentation analyst.
8. Money to pay a documentation analyst.
9. Printing facilities for documentation production and binding.
10. Money to pay for printing and binding.
11. Production facilities for a set of overhead foils for use at a users group.
12. Money to pay for the foils.
13. A contract to sell the system.
14. Money to pay legal fees for the contract.

John estimates his rough costs as attorneys' fees for test contract, $500; documentation fees, $1,000; printing costs ($5 per copy × 100), $500; foil costs ($5 per foil × 30), $150; and attorneys' fees for sales contract, $500.

John's total estimated costs are $2,650. He may have to pay additional fees to form his company, obtain a business license, hire an accountant, and so on, but for now he has come up with an initial estimate. As he is educated regarding additional needs, additional costs will become obvious. If John doesn't have sufficient money, he should not give up. Rather he should rework his plan to reduce his initial cash needs. He might be able to entice the documentation analyst to work on a royalty basis, with fees paid as the product is sold. He could have only one legal agreement drafted covering both testing and sales. He may be able to convince the attorney to defer collection for a period of time. Furthermore, John may be able to reduce computer output size to 8½ × 11, which he can run through a Xerox type copier to make foils.

However, without this rudimentary analysis, John may be in financial trouble. He may have other problems as well. As we shall see, by using his employer's computer to develop a system even with his employer's knowledge, John may be giving up ownership. Thus, he may need to find an outside computer resource. If John is clever, he may be able to trade his product for computer time, thus reducing financial requirements. Even if John does have the money to pay for these services, he should still consider finding an alternative; by so doing he can maximize profit. In most start-up companies cash is a scarce resource and is to be protected.

John's nonfinancial requirements are ascertainable. As he gets into his effort, he may discover there are certain required technical resources for which he did not initially plan. For example, he may discover that he needs to develop a special program to handle new disk formats. He can then add to his plan to supply those technical needs.

Judy, however, has extensive information and technical needs. She must perform detailed market research to design her system. She plans to follow the initial IMS release with a CICS version. Therefore, she needs access to technical documentation, installed systems software, and programming skills.

Joe may have to undertake additional hardware expenses and may wish to negotiate his discount first and then implement the system on hardware that is most favorable financially.

Most of this chapter has been devoted to examples showing defining of goals and objectives and then determining how to accomplish those objectives. This is a fundamental planning process. The final derived plan may change. In fact, we'll follow our illustrative plans through this book. The important fact is that before the first visit to an attorney, before the first conscious business effort, and before the first real activity, the software entrepreneur has developed a plan which becomes the fundamental working document of the effort.

2.3 VIEW OF THE PROCESS

Before continuing, we should note that there are really two ways to view the entrepreneurial process. The first is to look at the individual items that go into the process and examine each of these in detail in the order in which they occur. The second is to view the entire effort as a structured process utilizing a top–down approach. This structured approach is a very effective way of focusing the entire effort on the ultimate goal(s); however, it is not used in this book for the simple reason that we are focusing on tools and methods rather than a final implementation plan. It is very useful to examine this process from both points of view. In Figure 2.18, we have provided a T-chart for the

T-Chart — Entrepreneurial Process
MAXIMIZE PROFIT

Goals & Objectives	How
1. Initial plan	
2. Forming a business	
3. Detailed planning	
4. Formulate product ideas	
5. Project plans	
6. Implementation	
7. Testing	
8. Marketing	
9. Sales planning	
10. Presales effort	
11. Sales	
12. Sales management	
13. Support	
14. Follow-on business	
15. The reward	

FIGURE 2.18

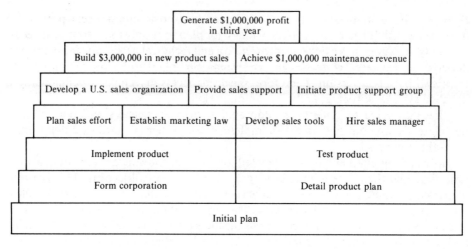

FIGURE 2.19   Structured top-down approach

process methodology. The reader should fill in the "How" column as each chapter is completed. Figure 2.19 is a top–down view of the entrepreneurial effort. By restating these processes after completion of this book, the reader can develop a working top-down model of his or her own effort.

—————————— R E V I E W ——————————

1. Take your own business enterprise and prepare a T-chart for it.

2. After you have completed the chart, write out a one-paragraph narrative for each item.

3. List out all requirements for your T-chart. Are they technical, informational, or monetary?

4. Refine your monetary requirements by estimating your rough costs. Are they realistic? Do you have enough money to finance this effort?

5. Make a list of questions that the T-chart creates.

6. Review the T-charts for John Jones, Judy Smith, and Joe Brown. What have they forgotten? What would you do differently?

7. Sit down with a friend or an associate to discuss the items on your T-chart, your narrative, and estimated costs. Revise them if necessary.

REFERENCES

This chapter was designed to help you verbalize your ideas. As we shall see, there are many excellent treatises on planning. The following are useful, introductory references.

1. Ackoff, Russel L., *A Concept of Corporate Planning*. New York: John Wiley & Sons, 1970. A fundamental treatise on planning, written with a management science flair and oriented more toward existing companies.

2. Uris, Auren, *The Executive Deskbook*. New York: Van Nostrand Reinhold Company, 1970. This is a very useful introductory reference to management techniques.

3. White, Richard M., *The Entrepreneur's Manual*. Radnor, Pa., Chilton Book Co., 1977. A general manual for new business start-ups which provides a great deal of food for thought for the would-be entrepreneur. Since this is non-industry-specific, some of the material is not applicable to the computer software industry.

Chapter 3

BUSINESS ENTITIES
How to Understand What You Are
Doing to Yourself

3.1 PROFESSIONAL ADVICE

With a rough plan for the business activity, the software entrepreneur must then proceed to form the business entity. There are two firm rules associated with this effort.

First, unless you are an attorney or an accountant, seek professional advice in forming a business. There are inexpensive publications which describe partnership and corporate formation. Although these are reasonable guides as to the "how to," they usually do not attempt to provide more than the basic facts. Software companies are strange beasts and the financial results of an error can be quite high.

The second rule is that this chapter is not a substitute for professional advice. However, by studying this material you can intelligently participate in the business formation process.

3.2 THE SOFTWARE COMPANY MODEL

Normally a guide to new business ventures begins with a description of the forms of business: sole proprietorship, partnership, and corporation. Before we discuss these forms per se, we will look at a software business transaction as a model for the various forms.

In a normal case, someone has designed and developed a software package which in turn is licensed to an end user for some lump sum payment. Note the word "license." This is the first clue that there is something different about software as opposed to hardware. You may believe that software is a physical good. Most tax courts believe this. However, there is still doubt that software can be protected from competitors and unscrupulous users in the same manner as hardware. Thus software is usually licensed to a single user. This is a license to use and does not transfer ownership. We'll discuss the concept of "intellectual property" later in this book. This distinction between hardware and software is very important to both you and your professional advisors. Additionally (and usually optionally) the end user pays a yearly maintenance fee. The concept of maintenance is essential to the structure of a software entrepreneurial venture. It represents a continuing obligation and a source of revenue.

If we greatly simplify the software enterprise, we see that we have certain key events.

1. Develop a product. (Normally little if any revenue until this process is completed.)
2. Begin to sell the product. (Usually a one-time license fee; sometimes a rental or leaselike periodic payment structure.)
3. Provide maintenance. (Typically a yearly charge is assessed.)
4. Provide enhancements. (Perhaps at a fee.)

These events are interwoven throughout the history of the company. It is important that the entrepreneur and legal and financial counsel understand these transactions prior to making the fundamental structuring decisions.

We'll now try to map this model onto one of our case studies. Let's look at Case B in the previous chapter.

Assume for a moment that business entities such as corporations or partnerships do not exist. Judy Smith could pay her programmers and other expenses out of her personal checking account. Any contracts for her software package would be directly between Judy Smith and the purchaser. Judy would deposit license fees in her personal checking account. Without some very creative tax planning, Judy would treat the license fees in a similar manner as her salary. She would treat her business expenses as deductions. She would provide maintenance and deposit maintenance fees. In essence, at the end of every year she would pay taxes based on income received and expenses *paid out*.

If Judy's product failed, the purchaser might choose to sue her. If Judy needed to borrow money, she would go to the bank and, on the basis of her credit history, obtain a loan.

In reality, this is not a terrible way for an individual to operate provided he or she maintains records and controls. It might not be the best structure as far as tax planning is concerned. Where this really breaks down, however, is with several participants.

In the case described, Judy controls the company. Although she may have employees, she is the owner. But what happens if Judy's programmers want some ownership? Of course Judy could offer them profit sharing and decision making based on a contract. Yet this is not really ownership.

Another difficulty comes when Judy desires to attract investors. Most investors wish to *own* a piece of the company in which they invest. The reason for this is that, as Judy's business grows, it will increase in value. As we will see later, value is related to but not limited to profit. These investors certainly do not want to be liable to the users for problems with the system.

The solutions to these problems are part of an overall scheme of legal business entities. State legislatures have passed laws permitting the formation of special business arrangements with certain characteristics and the federal government has created special tax treatment for these organizations. In spite of the negative implications of taxes, in some cases those laws are actually designed to stimulate business growth. With this in mind we will begin to examine the basic business entities.

3.3   BUSINESS FORMS

There are three basic forms of business: the sole proprietorship, the partnership, and the corporation. As we examine each of these, we will revise our elementary model as an illustration.

3.3.1   Sole Proprietorship

In the sole (or individual) proprietorship there is one individual owner, who may employ workers. In most states the sole proprietor can begin operation by obtaining a business license and complying with a few legal formalities. In our case, we have seen that the entrepreneur may operate this way by using her personal checking account to deposit funds as if she were receiving a salary and to pay for bills. (However, from a business standpoint even a sole proprietor should set up a separate checking account.) She could, by filing a fictitious business statement as required by state law, operate as A Enterprises and have a checking account in that name.

There are some distinct advantages to this form of business:

1. The owner is *the* decision maker and may move at a fast pace without delays or formalities.
2. There are very few legal requirements such as maintaining business notes or filing articles with government agencies.
3. The cost of forming a business is minimized.
4. The owner is the only one (if she so chooses) who can obligate the business to contracts or to debt.
5. The business can normally operate in other states without additional extensive legal requirements.

6. Regulations are minimal.
7. The owner may borrow funds or obtain credit on her total holdings rather than on the business's holdings.
8. There is no double taxation as occurs with corporations. (We will explain this when we discuss corporations.)
9. In a start-up situation the individual may deduct her losses at an early stage. This may be advantageous if the individual also has a reasonable personal income.

However, there are some distinct disadvantages to the sole proprietorship:

1. There is a certain stigma attached to doing business with a sole proprietorship. Some large companies do not wish to deal with this business form.
2. The owner is subject to unlimited personal liability for the obligations of the business. For example, if another software firm claims the owner stole their package and successfully goes to court winning a large settlement, the owner will likely be required to pay damages from personal funds.
3. The proprietor is the only one who can act for the business unless she grants an agent power to act. In some cases, employees may not proceed to maximize profit with the proprietor's action.
4. The capital available to the business is a function of the owner's resources and her ability to obtain those resources. Whereas a corporation that shows a history of growth might be looked at favorably by investors, the sole proprietorship normally is disfavored.
5. If the owner dies or is incapacitated, the business may dissolve.
6. All normal profits of the business are usually taxed as ordinary income to the owner, thus raising her tax bracket.
7. Because of the income tax on all normal profits, the individual may find it difficult to retain profits (tax free) to build her business.
8. It is very difficult to involve others in ownership.

The major reason that software entrepreneurs operate as sole proprietors is that this is a natural mode closely resembling their current personal financial operation. They can name the company if they so desire and by filing some minimal documents begin business. The major reason that software entrepreneurs should consider a sole proprietorship (or, as we shall see, a partnership) is that in certain instances the tax savings to the entrepreneur may be very dramatic. We'll examine this possibility later on.

Before leaving the sole proprietorship we should mention that some states have special provisions for one-person corporations. For purposes of this discussion, we'll treat these as normal corporations, noting that if such one-person corporations can be formed they usually require some but not all of the corporate formalities.

3.3.2 *Partnerships*

The second major form of business is the partnership. In our example, two individuals, Programmer and Analyst, could decide to go into business together, have an attorney draft a partnership agreement, comply with certain specific state requirements, and operate as P–A Associates. All contracts would be in the name of P–A Associates and a checking account would normally be set up for P–A Associates.

The normal attributes of a partnership are that usually any one partner may act on behalf of the business unless precluded from so doing by the partnership. There is usually liability on the part of each partner for all business obligations even if only one partner acted to incur the obligation. Unanimous consent is required to add additional partners, and the partnership usually dissolves on the death of a partner or the unilateral withdrawal of a partner. Additionally, the law of partnerships creates the concept of a fiduciary duty of each partner to display good faith, loyalty, and fairness in all partnership dealings.

Because of the nature of a partnership (even if the partnership agreement precludes such an agreement), the entity may be required to fulfill a contract entered into by a partner, if the other party has a reasonable belief that the partner is operating within the normal scope of the business. Thus one individual normally has authority to enter into a contract. For example, if P–A Associates enters into a contract with Customer to license Product and only P agrees to this, then even if P–A Associates' agreement is that both P and A must sign all contracts, it is likely that P–A would be bound.

There are some very important advantages to a partnership:

1. The legal formalities of operation are less than with a corporation. Thus, operation is simplified.
2. The cost of formation is normally less, although very detailed partnership agreements designed to accomplish specific tax or business purposes may be very costly.
3. Nonpartner employees cannot obligate the partnership for debt.
4. There is relatively little intrastate regulation on business operations.
5. Regulatory and reporting requirements are less than those for a corporation.
6. There is normally a cumulative borrowing effect, with a lending institution considering all the partners' wealth.

There are some very specific tax consequences of a partnership. The Internal Revenue Code, through Subchapter K, views the partnership as an "aggregate" entity. This means that effectively all profits and losses are passed to the individual partners. (That is, the partnership is not taxed but rather the partners are.) However, it is an entity for partnership transactions such as salary, investment, and so on. We will use our examples to help clarify this dual role.

P–A Associates would file an income tax return showing not only operating results but also the allocation of income, credit, deductions, and the like to each partner. This is an information-only report since the partnership does not pay taxes. Rather Programmer and Analyst include in their own income their allocation of income, losses, and deductions that have been passed through them by the partnership.

It should be pointed out that the IRS can and sometimes does challenge the status of a partnership and attempt to tax it as a corporation. The entrepreneur should realize that the IRS often will attempt to view the business entity in terms that maximize taxes. Thus, it is important that the partnership agreement and the operation of a partnership be carried out in the proper manner. The partners must consult with legal counsel in drafting their agreement and must adhere to the requirements of that agreement.

There are some disadvantages to a general partnership:

1. The life of a partnership is limited by agreement. Thus, it is entirely conceivable that the business entity may cease to exist before *all* of the partners wish.
2. Due to the tax nature of a partnership, additional tax reporting forms (and the concurrent expenses) are required.
3. Each partner, in general, has unlimited *personal* liability for all partnership obligations including those incurred by another partner. For example, if Analyst enters into a contract with Customer agreeing to be responsible for losses incurred by Customer due to failure of P–A's product and the product brings down Customer's teller information system, the Customer could win a one million dollar damage suit. Programmer is jointly liable for this claim.
4. Partnerships, by their nature, require mutual cooperation and are less responsive to individuality than other business entities.

Like sole proprietorships, partnerships can be an attractive business entity to software firms.

The liability of the partners is a very important disadvantage of the normal partnership and thus a special form of partnership—a *limited partnership*—is often utilized to overcome some of the liability concerns. A limited partnership is a partnership formed by two or more persons with one or more general partners and one or more limited partners. The limited partner is not bound by the obligations of the partnership.

The advantages of this form, in addition to those of a partnership, are:

1. The limited partner's liability for his participation is limited to the amount of his investment in the partnership.
2. A limited partnership does not cease to exist when a limited partner dies or becomes incapacitated.
3. A limited partner may, under proper circumstances, assign his partnership interest.
4. Minimal formality is required in most states.

The disadvantages of a limited partnership are:

1. The limited partnership must comply with more state laws in order to retain the "limited" aspects of the partnership. Failure to do so will cause unlimited liability for all partners.
2. There must be a general partner. If no one is willing to assume the risks, there cannot be a limited partnership.
3. A limited partner usually must not actively participate in the management of the business.
4. A limited partnership may be attacked by the Internal Revenue Service as an association and taxed under corporate laws.

Often, the general partner is a corporation. In order to prevent a sham transaction whereby the general partner corporation is really an extension of the partners, the IRS has adopted guidelines (which may vary over time) stating that the limited partners' direct or indirect ownership of the corporate general partner must not exceed a certain percentage and that corporate net worth must bear a stated relationship to the partnership's worth.

Limited partnerships have recently gained great favor as a vehicle for financing business ventures. The principals in the business are the general partners and the investors are the limited partners. Not only can the investors share in the profits, but in some cases they can immediately deduct their investment as a business expense. As we shall see later in this book, current tax laws tend to encourage research and development activities by the above mechanism. Thus the software entrepreneur may choose a limited partnership form with which to do business.

Related to a partnership is a *joint venture,* which is an association of entities formed for some mutual purpose. The joint venture is created by contract whereby all participants share in profits and losses, control of the venture, and joint proprietary interests. In general, one joint venturer may obligate the other participants. The joint venture is not a permanent entity. It is, quite simply, a contract between several business entities describing mutual operations. However, if Programmer decides to enter into a contract with Salesperson whereby Salesperson will sell Programmer's product, a form of joint venture is created. In actuality, the concept of a joint venture is often psychologically motivated to pull together several groups according to contractual standards. The participants remain, for all practical purposes, individual entities. Therefore a joint venture is not really a business entity but rather a business method.

3.3.3 Corporations

A corporation is actually a physical legal entity. In the eyes of the law, a corporation may act in a manner similar to an individual—by entering into contracts, etc. The shareholders of a corporation elect a board of directors to manage the corporation. Normally the Board of Directors appoints officers to care for the day-to-day activities, but remains very active, particularly in a new company. Note that since the shareholders elect the board members, the owners, in effect, may choose to have only themselves on the board. Most entrepreneurs prefer to have several outside board members. Remember, your attorney can advise you on the proper relationships and workings of a corporation.

To form the corporation PAS Incorporated, Programmer, Analyst, and Salesperson could (and should) consult with an attorney who will prepare Articles of Incorporation, Bylaws of the Corporation, and certain stock purchase agreements. Normally the Articles describe the corporate purpose and the type and amount of stock. The Bylaws describe the operation of the corporation. The stock purchase agreements define who will invest initially and usually are subject to approval at a formal meeting of the corporation. All three documents must comply with state law.

In some cases the attorney will first reserve a name for the corporation in one or more states. Once the name is reserved, the attorney will file the required documents, order a Corporate Minute Book, stock certificates, and Corporate Seal, and upon notification of the filing, hold the first meeting of the corporation. These activities can be done without an attorney. However, although many self-help publications claim the contrary, the attorney can provide some valuable assistance. Unless the entrepreneur is also an attorney or has formed and run several previous corporations, he or she is ill-advised to utilize self-help.

There are certain specific advantages to a corporation:

1. There is a psychological status to a corporation implying size and strength.
2. Shareholders have limited liability as to the debts of the corporation. There are some exceptions to this based on state laws such as full liability for the price of their stock, statutory liability for wages and taxes due, and personal liability if a creditor is able to "pierce the corporate veil." This latter term is a legal concept whereby a creditor would claim a fraudulent transaction or inadequate capitalization (i.e., initial investment) and obtain a judgment against a shareholder. The "piercing of the veil" concept literally defeats the limited liability of a corporation. However, if a shareholder adheres to the statutory requirements for corporate operation and does not utilize the corporation to operate in a fraudulent manner, he or she will normally not be liable for any corporate acts.
3. Ownership in the corporation (that is, stock) is usually freely transferable subject to federal and state securities law requirements and possible corporate restrictions.
4. A corporation's life is not dependent on the life of a shareholder.
5. A corporation is an autonomous legal entity and may acquire or sell property, enter into contracts, and participate in legal actions.
6. A corporation permits the investment of several investors in a common project. These investors do not have to share management tasks or incur personal liability.
7. There is a lower tax rate on corporate income than on individual income.

8. The corporation may retain (not distribute) all of its income in order to reinvest in the business.

There are also disadvantages to the corporate form:

1. The credit of the corporation is a function of its own assets and thus may yield limited borrowing power unless the investors agree to guarantee loans.
2. Since stock is readily transferable, "unfriendly" shareholders may be present. (This situation can usually be minimized through buy/sell agreements.)
3. The majority of stockholders may determine a course of action that is incompatible with the goals of smaller shareholders. However, minority shareholders do have some legal protection against fraudulent or overly oppressive majority action as a function of state law.
4. In most large corporations, unless there is a truly contested controversy, most voting is a rubber stamp approval of management.
5. Management of a corporation is separated from ownership. Theoretically, Programmer, Analyst, and Salesperson could form PAS Incorporated, continue to work at their present jobs, and hire President to manage PAS Corporation.
6. A corporation must "qualify" to do business in states other than that in which it is originally formed. Such qualification requires formal filings which are costly and time-consuming.
7. There are numerous governmental controls, restrictions, and reporting requirements on a corporation.
8. Corporations cannot qualify for capital gains or losses. As we shall see, this is a very important concept.
9. The corporation and its shareholders are subject to double taxation. The corporation's income is taxed and the shareholder is taxed on dividends received.
10. If a group of shareholders such as the investors own a majority of the corporation and thus control it, they may choose to replace the management. This obviously is a concern for the entrepreneur.

A related entity, which is a form of corporation, is the *closed corporation.* Although definitions of this form of business vary from state to state, there is normally an identity between the persons active in the corporation and those doing business. Since the specifics of this entity are a function of state law, we will not dwell on this form other than to point out that such a form exists and a start-up, small business may wish to consider this approach in order to minimize legal formalities if the applicable state law so allows.

There is another special form of corporation referred to as a *Subchapter S corporation,* which derives its name from Subchapter S of the 1954 Internal Revenue Code as revised in 1958. This corporation operates in a manner similar to a regular corporation. In order for a business to qualify as a Subchapter S corporation, several specific attributes must be present. These are detailed in Sections 1371 through 1378 of the Internal Revenue Code and must be rigidly adhered to. The principal attributes are:

1. The corporation may not be a subsidiary of another corporation nor may it own 80 percent of another active corporation.
2. Because it is based on a concept of limited shareholders, there may be only 15 or fewer shareholders in a Subchapter S corporation.
3. There may only be one class of stock issued by the corporation.

These and the other attributes are very rigidly construed, and in no case should an entrepreneur attempt to form a Subchapter S corporation without professional legal and tax accounting advice.

The Internal Revenue Code permits the Subchapter S corporation to file an informational return to to tax the income and loss to the shareholders. Thus, if a Subchapter S corporation earns $1,000 and distributes $800 to a shareholder yet retains $200 for corporate growth, the shareholder is taxed on the $800 in the year in which he or she receives it and the $200 at the end of the corporate fiscal year. However, operating losses are passed on to shareholders subject to special rules and are limited to the basis (or investment) of the stock and loans to the corporation. The Subchapter S corporation thus has some of the advantages of both a corporation and a partnership.

There is a major difference of opinion among tax professionals as to the value of Subchapter S corporations, since the tax consequences of disallowance of the Subchapter S qualification of certain transactions involving the sale of the corporate entity or its assets may be severe. However, a competent tax practitioner will be able to advise you as to the desirability of a Subchapter S election and you should examine the benefits and restrictions.

3.4 TAX CONSEQUENCES

The Internal Revenue Code, which governs federal tax laws, looks at business organizations in two ways. The first is how the income of the business is taxed to the owners of the business, as illustrated by our earlier example with Judy Smith's personal operation. The second taxes income first at the entity and then again when it is distributed to the owners.

The first form is considered a conduit or a pass-through and, for our analysis, we will use the P–A Associates partnership as a prototype.

The second form is a separate taxable entity, and for our analysis we will consider PAS Incorporated formed by Programmer, Analyst, and Salesperson.

P–A Associates must report its earnings to the government. However, P and A individually report their share of the income, whether or not they receive income payment from P–A Associates. If Programmer earns $30,000 per year working for XYZ

Corporation and his share of P–A Associates income is $15,000, his taxable income is $45,000.

If P–A Associates has $50,000 income after expenses, Programmer has no additional income, and Programmer and Analyst are equal partners, then Programmer would have a taxable income of $25,000. Assume that Programmer is married to a non-income-producing spouse and that his deductions offset his additional income. Based on 1979 tax rates and some simplifying assumptions, Programmer would pay $5,033 in tax, or an effective rate of 20.1 percent of his share of the partnership earnings.

PAS Incorporated must file its own tax return. The normal rate of tax paid by a corporation is usually less than an individual's. However, the effective rate is not clearly lower.

If Programmer worked for PAS Incorporated and drew a $25,000 salary, the same effect would occur. However, if he took only $20,000 salary, he would pay a federal tax of $3,225 for that salary. The corporation would pay a federal tax of $850 on the $5,000 remaining as profit. If PAS Incorporated pays Programmer a $4,150 dividend ($5,000 less $850 due to IRS) he would pay an additional $1,154 or a total of $4,379 in income tax. The total taxes paid would be $4,379 plus $850 or $5,229 (20.9 percent). This methodology pays the government an additional $196 at an effective rate of 20.9 percent. This illustrates the concept of double taxation. It is very important to note that earnings must eventually be distributed. The tax laws require dividends to be paid when a certain level of earnings are accumulated beyond those required for normal business working capital. Through the imposition of an accumulated earnings penalty the government penalizes a corporation that accumulates earnings and profits in excess of $150,000 if such accumulation is for tax avoidance. Thus through a negative penalty, there is a positive incentive to issue dividends.

Additionally, many new enterprises operate at a loss during their start-up years. Programmer can deduct his share of that loss by P–A Associates. However, if Programmer instead had formed PAS Incorporated, he could not personally take a deduction in the year the loss occurred and PAS Incorporated would offset future income with that loss.

Normally, if a corporation continued to lose money and eventually failed, causing the stock to become worthless, Programmer could deduct this loss as a capital loss. Such a capital loss is less favorable to the taxpayer than an ordinary loss.

One major tax-oriented organizational technique is Section 1244 stock. In order to assist small business shareholders, Congress in the 1978 Revenue Act created this special form of stock which allows a stockholder to treat a capital loss for such stock as an ordinary loss and thus achieve a much higher rate of deduction. There are certain requirements for stock to qualify as Section 1244 stock. If you form a corporation, be certain to see that your attorney considers this option, since the requirements are quite minimal and the benefits substantial.

We have alluded to capital gains taxation. For income tax purposes there are sales or transfers of two types of items, capital and ordinary. Capital goods normally have a finite useful life *and* are used and/or owned under certain conditions. In order to encourage capital investment, that is, investment in new equipment, the tax laws offer certain favorable treatment such as tax credits to capital goods. Additionally, because of the nature of capital goods, income derived from the sale or transfer of capital goods is taxed at a lower rate. Consequently, a loss incurred in the sale of capital goods is also treated in effect as a reduced loss and thus any credit against ordinary income is reduced.

Applying this concept to the software industry, many entrepreneurs have recognized an excellent tax savings potential. For our purposes we'll assume that software is a capital good and that Programmer has consulted with a tax accountant and an attorney to be certain software is so treated. Assume that Programmer has developed System and that he has held System for over one year. In *a properly structured transaction* Programmer can sell his ownership (all substantial rights) of System for $50,000 to PAS Incorporated, in which he owns less than 25 percent in value, and he can treat the $50,000 as a long-term capital gain. In fact, Programmer could transfer his ownership and receive royalties as a percentage of sales. These royalties could be taxed as a long-term capital gain and Programmer's taxes can be reduced.

This concept is used by many software authors to change highly taxed ordinary income into lower taxed capital gains. A good attorney, knowledgeable in tax law, and a good tax accountant can structure such a transaction.

The tax laws do not permit corporations to claim capital gains. In the above example, if a corporation sold System to PAS Incorporated, the $50,000 capital would be ordinary income to that corporation and taxed at a higher rate. This is a very important reason why one may not wish to form a corporation initially when product development begins. The entire area of tax planning is exceptionally important in entrepreneurship. Keep in mind that tax laws change, strict formalities must be observed, and the IRS maintains a large, aggressive, and competent legal staff to challenge faulty tax avoidance schemes. This is clearly an area in which you should seek professional legal and accounting advice.

With this background, how do you decide in what form of business you want to engage? First of all you must realize there are tax and legal consequences to your eventual choice. After reading this chapter, you should be able to speak intelligently with professionals who are paid to structure your business. Briefly, the tax consequences include:

1. Double taxation of corporations
2. Deductibility of early losses in some cases
3. The capital gains transaction to minimize taxation

The legal considerations include:

1. Formal reporting and compliance requirements
2. Limitation of personal liability
3. Operation of the business
4. Ability to attract investments and obtain loans

There are also emotional requirements. Your self-image may be such that you have always wanted to be president of a successful corporation. Or perhaps you and your associates want to be partners and you are unable to have anything other than absolute equality; even with careful structuring of a corporation, you may still not feel at ease with any form of business other than a partnership.

3.5 FINDING PROFESSIONALS

We've already emphasized that you should obtain assistance. How do you find competent attorneys and accountants? One way to begin is to ask friends and acquaintances for recommendations. Another way is to contact your local bar association and / or accounting association. A third source of references is the trade journals; note which professionals publish articles. Another source is your banker. You can also contact a local university and ask faculty members for referrals. Finally, you might call up local software firms and ask them whom they use and what their opinions are of those legal and accounting firms.

Once you have done that, you should set up a brief meeting with one or more professionals. Be prepared to spend ten to fifteen minutes explaining what you want to do. Try to determine if the professional knows anything about computers or, at the very least, understands what you're talking about. Then be prepared to answer a few questions. Finally, ask the professional a few questions such as: "Have you ever formed a similar company before?" "Can you give me client references?" "What will you charge me?" "Do you consider yourself qualified to offer tax planning advice?"

You are not obliged to engage the professional after this first meeting. He may charge you for the meeting, but you should be convinced he is qualified and, even more important, that you can work with him. The professional should be able to tell you the set fees for his services. He may charge you on an hourly basis, but he should be able to estimate the charges. If you do not have enough money to pay for his services at one time, you may be able to arrange to pay over a few months. Do not be overimpressed with his office surroundings, yet note if he seems to be organized and responsive. Remember, you are the client and the professional is offering a service to you. Don't be afraid to ask questions, and certainly insist on participating in the decisions.

It is very important to be comfortable with your accountant and attorney. Your accountant will, in some ways, serve as your alter ego, often asking embarrassing questions or pointing out defects. Yet this same person can be very helpful, particularly when you wish to borrow money, raise capital, or minimize taxes. In a like manner your attorney often is privy to your basic business motivations such as your limits with a contract. That attorney should be able to assist you in negotiations as well as in the business community.

In some cases, you may be happier dealing with a large accounting or legal firm. They normally have extensive resources. However, often their service is more expensive and less personalized. On the other hand, though a single practitioner can usually be more attentive, you may quickly go beyond that individual's abilities unless he or she is experienced in this type of work. The sign of a good professional is the willingness to refer you to another practitioner when unable to solve your problem in a cost-effective and timely manner. If you are unhappy with the results, tell the professional and, if necessary, obtain another opinion.

You may wish to engage a different practitioner to assist you in various phases of your business. For example, initially you may choose to use a tax and business planning legal specialist whereas later in your activities you may want someone more knowledgeable in the law as it is specifically related to computers. Initially you may desire an accounting firm to set up your books whereas later on you may require a formal auditor.

An attorney is very similar to a programmer in that he or she may have specialties. There is some merit to finding legal counsel with specialties in tax and business planning, computer-related law, and, in some cases, general business law. In most large cities you can find such an individual.

As a side note, there is a Computer Law Association as well as an American Bar Association subcommittee dealing with computer law. If your legal professional does not belong to either of these, he or she may not be current with many of the aspects of computer law necessary to help you. In fact, there are law firms that specialize in computer-related law. If you have to choose between a good attorney without computer knowledge and an unresponsive, yet computer-knowledgeable individual, choose the good attorney. But why not try to get both?

Obviously, you should also consult with financial professionals. Many recently trained accountants are familiar with data processing, and this is helpful. They should also know generally accepted accounting practices related to software companies.

There are three general types of financial professionals: certified, public, and bookkeepers. Certified accountants are degreed and, after certain work requirements and test requirements, are licensed. The principal advantage of a certified public accountant is that he or she may certify a financial statement after audit. Such certification is often necessary for varying uses. Public accountants normally are degreed and well trained. Bookkeepers, as their name suggests, provide bookkeeping services. All three serve very useful functions.

The same selection criteria hold true with accountants as with attorneys. If you plan to obtain outside financing and may eventually wish to sell your stock to a large number of investors, it's probably a good idea to use a CPA, at least to help you set up an accounting system. Often you will not prepare audited statements until after a few years. However, by starting out with a good system you can minimize the cost and effort. When you select your accounting professional you should be prepared to ask many questions. You will maintain company books not only to know your status but also to pay taxes. In fact, a good financial system will enable you to manage your business. There is a big difference between the financial controls required for a software company and those required for a manufacturing company. Be certain your financial professional recognizes this difference and can also provide you with fundamental financial control and analysis tools.

One bit of advice: be certain your attorney and your accountant talk to one another. Don't be surprised that there may be more than one way to solve the same financial or legal problem. It's a good idea to have both your attorney and accountant review these decisions. However, remember, in any case, that you are the decision maker.

3.6 A CASE STUDY

We will emphasize some of the points in this chapter, by looking at Case C—Joe Brown, the entrepreneurial mechanical engineer.

Joe wishes to sell a combined hardware and software system. In order to do this, he will have to invest in the purchase of hardware. Additionally, because of his chosen sales methodology, he will be signing a lease for showroom space. Finally, he wants his company to establish a national reputation. Since Joe's system will be used by structural engineers to analyze designs, there may be very dramatic consequences of an improperly working system. These items tend to point toward a corporation as Joe's vehicle. On the other hand, Joe will likely have to guarantee any purchases or loans. Additionally, due to the purchase of capital equipment, there will be depreciation and investment credit tax advantages. These indicate that, at least during development, Joe may wish to be able to deduct these expenses from personal income.

Let's assume that Joe consults some creative attorneys and accountants who suggest the following:

1. Joe develops the initial system as a partnership, JB Limited. He will be the general partner, and he and two others will invest in this development.
2. Joe forms JB Computers, Inc., which will sell the system based on a grant from JB Limited to JB Computers, Inc., with JB Limited receiving royalties.
3. JB Limited issues a research contract to JB Computers, Inc., to design and develop the system.
4. The investors (and probably Joe) can write off development costs (based on proper structuring).
5. Any royalties to JB Limited are taxed as capital gains.

This structure is not uncommon for many new entrepreneurial ventures. The actual execution of this plan requires an acute awareness of Internal Revenue Service guidelines as well as state securities regulations. The structure is not the answer for everyone, but in Joe's case it is very useful, because Joe has obtained investment capital and provided a means for his investors to write off their investment as well as receive a payback in the form of capital gains. Additionally, the major risk of liability due to product failure has been absorbed through JB Computers, Inc., which, because of its corporate structure, will certainly protect the investors and likely protect Joe.

Without proper guidance, the software entrepreneur may not only miss opportunities for creative planning, but also penalize the business enterprise.

───────────────────────── **REVIEW** ─────────────────────────

1. Take three sheets of paper and head them Sole Proprietor, Partnership, and Corporation. As they apply to your venture, list the positive aspects on the left and negative aspects on the right of each sheet.

2. Review the software advertisements and announcements in industry publications. Are most of the organizations corporations? (Usually these have the words "Corporation" or "Incorporated" with them.) Is there a correlation between form and size?

3. Do you plan to work at your current job while you begin your entrepreneurial venture? If so, how will your current employer react? Does a special business form assist you in minimizing this potential conflict?

4. If your venture is with more than one person, answer the following:
    (a) Who will invest in the company and how much will be invested?
    (b) How and when will you split profits?
    (c) Do you each need a salary? Will it be equal?
    (d) Do you each have many personal assets?
    (e) If you each choose to go your own way, how will you split the company?

5. Explain the concept of double taxation. How does it apply to your venture?

6. Prepare a checklist of questions for prospective attorneys and accountants.

7. Call the president of one or two local software firms. Tell them that you are about to begin a company. Ask them to recommend a legal firm and an accounting firm.

8. Obtain and read the annual reports of publically traded software firms. Pay particular attention to the notes explaining the accounting procedures.

REFERENCES

There are two classes of reference materials on business formation, *introductory* and *detailed*. Volumes of each type are available. After you choose an attorney and an accountant, ask each to provide you with some suggested reading.

If you understand this chapter and desire more advanced texts, the following is a list of a few excellent ones.

General Business Entities

1. Giacomini, Edward, John O. Hargrove, and Winslow O. Small, *Organizing Corporations in California*. Berkeley, Cal.: California Continuing Education of the Bar, 1973. (Supplemented Annually) This is an excellent how-to treatise used by many California attorneys. Similar volumes are available in other states.

2. Rohrlich, Chester, *Organizing Corporate and Other Business Enterprises*. New York: Matthew Bender, 1980. This is a very comprehensive legal reference book which is used by many attorneys. It not only reviews major issues but also provides additional references. Its format is such that it is an excellent follow-on to this chapter.

Taxation

1. Cavitch, Zolman, *Tax Planning for Corporations and Shareholders*. New York: Matthew Bender, 1980. This is a detailed review of applicable federal tax law as related to corporations and should be referred to for unanswered tax considerations. (As noted, tax law is very complicated and a professional should be consulted *prior* to individual research.)

2. Prentice-Hall Editorial Staff, *Federal Tax Course 1980*. Englewood Cliffs, N.J.: Prentice-Hall, Inc., 1980. A very easy to understand and detailed guide to taxation of individuals, partnerships, and corporations, this book is updated annually, is used by many tax practitioners, and is a fundamental handbook for anyone concerned with taxation.

Chapter 4

BEGINNING DETAILED PLANNING
How to Know What to Do Now That You Know What You Are

4.1 FACILITIES

By now, the entrepreneur will have a rough idea of the business activity and the form of business entity. The entrepreneur ultimately requires a business plan. We will discuss business plans here and detail them in Appendix A. One very important input to this plan is the facilities requirements for the new venture.

Unless you have a written agreement with your current employer stating that you may use his facilities for furtherance of your business activities, you should plan to have a physical space outside of your place of employment in which to work. The reason for this is that in most cases an employer who can show your use of his facilities to develop a product may have a valid ownership interest in a product.

If you are a person who can work at home in a productive manner, you may be able to avoid the cost of an office. There are several disadvantages to an in-home office, not the least of which is the distraction element. Additionally, you may not have access to the facilities you need to complete your work. The primary advantage to working at home is cost savings, with a possible secondary advantage of family comfort. Normally, a valid in-home office qualifies for some tax deductions and, in spite of the Internal Revenue Service's very aggressive scrutiny (often including tax audit), this may prove of value. Thus, the requirements and consequences of deduction of office-at-home expenses are a complicated tax matter which often changes with new Internal Revenue Rulings. You should consult a tax accountant or attorney before planning on or claiming such a deduction.

For an office in the home, you should at the very least have a desk, a good lamp, a comfortable chair, a file cabinet, some shelves, adequate storage space, and other supplies. A private business telephone and a good answering service or machine is best. Finally, privacy is essential. Caring for your young child is really not a profit-oriented task when you are supposed to be preparing sales materials. An additional point is that as you develop your company you may require a business address, particularly if you are going to deal with larger companies. Most larger cities have offices that provide mail-receiving and somtimes conference facilities. Many software entrepreneurs have effectively run million dollar businesses from their homes with the use of such offices. It's really up to you to decide if this is an effective way to do business. It can work but it requires discipline.

If you choose to open an office outside of your home, there are numerous considerations. Before looking for office space, it is best to prepare a budget. The price of usable office space varies greatly with location, facilities, and service. There are two major ways to obtain office space. The first is the rental or lease of an office which normally includes the space, walls "as is," carpeting, and a few fixtures such as lights, curtains, and wall plugs. The other basic method is to rent space in a suite from a service; if you choose, you may move into a furnished office which provides, among other things (usually at an additional charge), secretarial services, copiers, postage meters, an answering service, a receptionist, a lobby, and a conference room. The best way to find out about both types of offices is to consult the classified advertisements and the telephone yellow pages under "Offices" or "Secretarial Services." As a rule of thumb, you will pay about twice as much for a service suite space as a raw office and the charges for services will normally be 25 to 50 percent higher than bargain rates. However, service suites are very convenient and time-saving. Many computer software firms use this alternative for field sales and support offices, as do many start-up operations.

There are numerous factors to consider in the selection of office space:

1. *Geographic convenience.* If you are going to continue working full-time, is the facility convenient to your home and/or work? If you plan to work only at your new venture, is the location convenient for you and those who may visit you?

2. *Used facilities.* If you plan to hide away and work, as opposed to having frequent visitors and guests, the prestige of a location is usually unimportant. If you do expect to have others meet with you, you should recognize that your office is a reflection of you. In the former case, a comfortable, quiet office is sufficient. In the latter case, you may desire a reception area and fancier surroundings.

3. *Required services.* If you plan to use a commercial computer service to develop your system, you may wish to be located near that service. (Some commercial computer services may provide office space as part of their package. You should examine this possibility.) You may need daily, as opposed to occasional, access to a word-processing system or a print shop.

4. *Access to building.* Most software entrepreneurs do not work from 9 to 5. Be certain you can get into the office during odd hours and be certain that the security in the building enables you to feel safe in doing so. Also remember that air conditioning and heat may not be provided 24 hours a day.

5. *Parking.* You should determine if there are parking facilities, and if so, their cost and ease of use. Many an entrepreneur is surprised to find that an additional charge of $50 to $100 per month per car is added to the bill.

6. *Support services.* If you do not use a service suite, are there convenient secretarial and copying services nearby?

Once you have decided on space, if it is unfurnished, you should budget for furnishing it. Usually you will need the same equipment as at home except that you may wish to obtain more impressive items. These include a desk and/or work table, a file cabinet, a bookcase, a stand for a terminal if you use one, a comfortable work chair, and one or two guest chairs. Even if the office is furnished, you will need to supply additional items.

The cost for these items is usually a function of your creativity and your need for an image. You can furnish an office for under $150 if you can settle for used furniture and supplement the office with items from home. In general, you want the office to be as comfortable *to you* as possible so as to allow you to work in an efficient manner. The basic rule is comfort for the least price unless you expect many visitors, in which case you probably want a better image. You may wish to rent furniture or to buy new furniture, depending on the economics. You should look at the comparative costs.

Several of these items deserve special mention. When you obtain a file cabinet you must choose between letter, legal, or computer printout size. There is no magic rule, but a small two-drawer letter size file cabinet with a lock is usually sufficient. When you order your telephone you should consider how it will be used. Will you need more than one line and if so, do you need a rotary? Perhaps special features are available that can eliminate the expense of an additional line. Phone installations are expensive and proper planning is required. Stationery and business cards are very important for marketing and sales; they are less important for pure development activities. A general rule of thumb is that if your initial activity will be limited to nonsales and marketing functions, you should be able to use less expensive, standard business stationery without a special logo. Once you begin to communicate with investors or clients, you may wish to have a commercial artist help you prepare a more professional image. Stationery is not inexpensive and so you should be fairly confident that you will be at your business address and telephone number for some time in the future before ordering extensive quantities.

If you do not use a service suite, you should arrange for necessary support services. You may choose to do your own typing with either a typewriter or a letter-quality computer terminal. (Most computer users and marketers look with disdain at normal computer printer output used for business correspondence and marketing literature, so if you're going to use a computer for those functions, be certain that the quality is equivalent to or better than a normal carbon ribbon business typewriter.) If you wish to purchase or rent a typewriter, be certain that it is a quality one. There is nothing wrong with purchasing a used typewriter or a less expensive portable model if it produces crisp, clear copy.

As for copier services, many facilities are available. The acceptable "out-of-office" document is on bond or letter-quality paper and not the less expensive, chemically treated glossy copies. Usually a quality copy can be made for a reasonable price. It's worth it.

If you use an answering service or answering machine, be very conscious of quality. Most answering services cannot give you the same attention that a personal secretary can. Check with your friends or, if you must, use the yellow pages to find a service. Ask for references and do not be afraid to check the service. If your clients are placed on hold for 20 or more seconds every time they call and if the service mispronounces your name, you have a real problem. An answering machine is a viable alternative. There are some people who hate these devices, and that fact can affect your clients. However, such machines are now generally acceptable. Shop around, considering features and costs. Determine if you really need remote access or if you can wait until you come into the office for messages. Remember, if you purchase such a machine you will likely replace it only when it stops functioning, so consider your personal needs.

Additionally, if you have your own equipment and furniture, you may require general liability, theft, and fire insurance. You should consult several insurance agents to determine your needs and then make up your mind. If you are not employed elsewhere, you may wish to obtain life and health care insurance. Again, talk to several agents and make up your own mind as to needs.

4.2 PREPARING A BUDGET

Now that you have determined your needs to get started, you should prepare a budget. There are two basic reasons for preparing a budget. First (and most obvious), the budget is *the* fundamental tool with which entrepreneurs manage their business. Second, the budget is a necessary ingredient to a formal business plan.

This budget should be on a monthly basis and you should project your costs for at least six months, and likely one year. This time span is required because there are basically three frequencies of costs. The first is a one-time charge, usually at start-up. Examples of this are telephone deposits and installation fees, legal fees to form your business, and so on. Others occur at a monthly interval. For example, rents are usually due monthly. Still others may occur periodically at various intervals. You may determine that your stationery will last for six months, at which time you will have to replenish it. Figure 4.1 illustrates a typical beginning budget. Naturally, this is hypothetical and your own cost items will vary. There are many items you will wish to add to your budget as we examine other aspects of software entrepreneurship. However, these budget items include most items discussed to this point.

Don't be afraid to review your budget with your financial advisor. Once you have

Item	1	2	3	4	5	6	7	8	9	10	11	12	Total
Legal Fees	$250	$250	—	—	—	—	—	—	—	—	—	—	$ 500
Accounting Fees	200	—	—	$100	—	—	$100	—	—	$100	—	—	500
Rent	300	150	$150	150	$150	$150	150	$150	$150	150	$150	$150	1,950
Telephone	300	100	100	100	100	100	100	100	100	100	100	100	1,400
Ans. Service	50	30	30	30	30	30	30	30	30	30	30	30	380
Furniture	250	250	0	0	0	0	0	0	0	0	0	0	500
Secretarial	100	100	100	100	100	200	200	200	200	200	200	200	1,900
Insurance	100	0	0	100	0	0	100	0	0	100	0	0	400
Stationery & Supplies	150	20	20	20	20	20	20	20	20	20	20	20	370
Postage	25	10	10	10	10	25	10	10	10	10	10	10	150
Licenses/ Taxes	100	100	50	50	50	50	50	50	50	50	50	50	700
Computer Equipment	200	100	100	100	100	100	100	100	100	100	100	100	1,300
Computer Services	0	100	100	100	100	100	100	100	100	100	100	100	1,100
Copies	20	20	20	20	20	20	20	20	20	20	20	20	240
Total	$2,045	$1,230	$680	$880	$680	$795	$980	$780	$780	$980	$780	$780	$11,390

FIGURE 4.1   Projected monthly budget (illustrative)

determined the costs, you should very quickly determine if you have sufficient cash flow to cover the expenses. Remember, the major factor in business failure is insufficient cash to meet expenses. The reason for insufficient cash is often undercapitalization. That is, many business failures result because a would-be entrepreneur does not have sufficient funds to carry on the business.

What if you have prepared an initial budget and you do not have the financial resources to bring it off? You have two alternatives. The first is to attempt to reduce the expenses. There are several ways of accomplishing this. First, you can simply use less expensive services, facilities, and supplies. Second, you can barter for services. This technique is exceptionally attractive if you plan to use an outside computer facility. Many installations will trade computer time for packages. In fact, they may be willing to supply, in addition to computer time, basic items such as office space or typing. If you do barter for time, formalize your agreement by having your attorney draft a contract.

A third technique is to raise money. There are several ways to do this, including self-financing, sponsor site financing, tax shelter financing, and venture capital. There are firms that specialize in providing financing to high-technology companies. However, the basic fact of life is that the chances are very slight of obtaining *start-up* financing without a track record of successful entrepreneurial ventures. Thus such an effort may be time-consuming and nonproductive. Therefore, the information on venture capital funding has been placed in the Appendix.

Self-financing is probably the most widely used method of start-up financing. It can be accomplished by combinations of two fundamental techniques—saving and borrowing. By changing your lifestyle and setting up a realistic personal budget, you can save money to finance your business venture. It is important to realize that you should be able to save a percentage of your current income for this purpose. In fact, if you are unwilling to change your lifestyle in order to get your business started, you are probably wasting your time. You might be surprised how many successful entrepreneurs go through dramatic lifestyle changes, trading social luncheons for brown bagging, new cars for repairs on an old one, movies for television, and so on. Additionally, many entrepreneurs use previously accumulated savings for self-financing.

The second fundamental self-financing technique is borrowing. There are numerous ways to borrow. Many start-ups are financed in part by utilizing credit lines tied into bank credit cards. Of course, you can go to a bank to borrow money. It's very likely that, unless you find a very progressive, aggressive (and perhaps foolish) banker, you cannot expect to borrow money without collateral or a co-signer. This usually means that you must have some personal assets such as a paid-for car, home equity, etc. to pledge as well as some previous history of credit-worthiness. If you are able to borrow some money, you should budget the payments.

Choosing your business banker is very important. You should not, except out of sheer necessity, walk into a bank and open an account without first discussing your business with a bank officer. If you have a good personal banking relationship, you may wish to discuss your business first with that bank. If not, your attorney or accountant should be able to recommend a bank. There are several factors in a successful banking relationship. First of all, some banks aggressively wish to handle business accounts. They advertise their business expertise and welcome new businesses. They may be more progressive in their lending policies and certainly can help you in some situations. Second, as with any business relationship, you should have a bank officer who knows you by name, who understands what you are trying to do, and with whom you can communicate. Third, there should be some convenience associated with the bank. Remember that a good banking relationship can be very important to your company. Successful entrepreneurs spend time establishing and maintaining this relationship.

A very creative method sometimes used for paying for development of software systems is sponsor site financing. The scenario for this type of activity is that the entrepreneur finds a small number (one to five) of companies who are willing to pay some percentage of the development cost and participate in the design of the actual system. Of course it helps if you have some friends at these installations who have faith in your venture. The details of such an arrangement vary, but usually include:

- Early delivery of a software system
- Some financial payment varying from a discounted final price to repayment to the sponsor of total development costs
- Supply of computer testing
- Willingness to be a reference site
- Participation in design and implementation review teams
- Some potential future financial remuneration of the sponsors

Sponsor site companies should be required to sign a detailed contract which covers not only the business details but also specific ownership issues to be certain that the software developer retains ownership of the product. The sponsor site methodology is a very useful technique for both financing and product input.

Tax shelter financing has recently come in vogue. We will discuss it briefly here, but the concept is detailed in Appendix A. Currently some computer software and hardware development activities are being financed by means of research and development (R & D) tax shelters. The concept is superficially easy to understand but difficult to implement. Do not attempt to create an R & D tax shelter without the guidance of experienced attorneys and accountants!

The superficial concept, illustrated in the previous chapter, is that a group of investors form a limited partnership which then issues a research and development contract to the software company (a separate entity). Usually the software company also receives total rights to the product in return for a royalty agreement which provides for the software company to pay royalties on sales to the limited partnership. If the arrangement is structured correctly, the partners of the partnership can immediately write off the research and development cost as ordinary expenses and treat the royalties as a long-term capital gain. There are some people who are experts at this type of financing. They can usually be found in high technology areas, and your accountant and attorney may be able to refer you to them.

Once you have prepared a budget and are comfortable with your financing, do not vary from your budget without careful analysis. For example, a memory typewriter might be more useful than a normal one, yet the extra cost may be the difference between survival and failure. The budget is a living document which requires revision and constant question.

The major point of this section is that you should not attempt to start your business unless you have adequate capital either on hand or available as needed. If you do begin without enough funding, you are fighting severe odds against success. Spend sufficient initial time to obtain the necessary capital. Remember that this planning effort is an integral part of your business plan.

4.3 A CASE STUDY

As a brief review, we will examine John Jones's business effort. He has already decided he wishes to leave his current employer. John has decided to approach his friend at the Contiguous Insurance Society, Inc., in order to trade JJCOPY for computer time. He decides to work out of his recreation room at home. He has put a plywood board over the pool table to create work space, purchased a used desk chair and a letter-quality printer plus a modem for his Apple computer. His six-month budget is shown in Figure 4.2.

Aside from the barter for computer time, John has made a few very interesting plans. These are as follows:

1. He will purchase some computer equipment.
2. He will purchase an answering machine.
3. He chooses to take a salary, which is necessary for his survival.
4. He will not initially purchase insurance, but will obtain it at a latter date.

Where does John get this money from? If he hasn't saved $16,920, he must find another source of funds. Perhaps he will continue to work to earn the money. Maybe he can borrow on the equity in his home. Obviously John plans to have income after month six that is equal or greater than expenses or else his needs will be greater. Only John knows if this is a feasible budget. His financial advisors can tell him if his assumptions are realistic. This is a necessary project for John and a part of his basic business success.

In summary, unless you commit to planning, you might as well take your funds and go to the nearest casino—the odds for random success are probably better there than in a software venture. With planning, the odds of success are really in your favor, and of course planning is an activity that by its very nature maximizes profit.

Item \ Month	1	2	3	4	5	6	Total
Legal Fees	$ 500	0	0	0	$ 250	0	$ 750
Accounting Fees	0	$ 500	0	0	0	0	500
Telephone	150	50	50	50	50	50	400
Ans. Machine	250	0	0	0	0	0	250
Furniture	100	0	0	0	0	0	100
Secretarial	0	0	100	100	100	100	400
Stationery & Supplies	100	50	50	50	200	50	500
Postage	25	25	25	25	25	25	150
Licenses/ Taxes	400	0	0	0	0	0	400
Computer Equipment	1,200	0	0	0	0	0	1,200
Computer Services	0	0	0	0	0	0	0
Copying	20	20	20	20	20	20	120
Artwork/ Slides	0	0	0	50	50	50	150
Salary	2,000	2,000	2,000	2,000	2,000	2,000	12,000
Total	$4,745	$2,645	$2,245	$2,295	$2,695	$2,295	$16,920

FIGURE 4.2   John Jones' projected monthly budget

REVIEW

1. Begin to plan for facilities by actually looking at office space. How much space do you require? What does it cost in your area?

2. Examine your house to see if you have sufficient space in which to work.

3. Visit office buildings with available space *before* you decide what you require.

4. Make a list of items you need for an office. Note special features you might want (such as an L-shaped desk)

5. Talk to office equipment salespeople and begin to review features. Also talk to secretaries at work about typewriters and word-processing equipment. What features do you need?

6. Review the sample budget (Figure 4.1) and determine what items have been left out. See if you can determine what expenses are totally out of line.

7. Prepare a budget for your venture. Review it and revise it.

8. How can you reduce your expenditures?

9. After talking to your advisors, meet a few bankers. Do they have special programs for new businesses?

REFERENCE

1. Bank of America NT & SA Marketing Department, "Financing Small Business," *Small Business Reporter,* vol. 14, no. 10 (1980). This is a very concise, well-written 33-page document which includes planning, financing, business plan, and other relevant advice. Every would-be software entrepreneur should read this document.

Chapter 5

PRODUCT DEFINITION
Do You Really Know What You Are Going to Do?

5.1 FORMULATING PRODUCT IDEAS

Most entrepreneurs already have a product idea. In some cases the idea is simply a gleam in someone's eye. For example, as in our original Case A, a clever systems programmer may recognize that a given IBM-supplied utility program could be vastly enhanced and the programmer may wish to rewrite that utility. In other cases, the entrepreneur may have already implemented a product idea. The IBM-supplied utility could be rewritten, installed, and made market ready, hopefully in a manner that not only is superior to the IBM utility but also avoids plagiarism. *Regardless of the status of the idea, the entrepreneur should utilize certain techniques for formulating product ideas.* These techniques are useful not only for creating new ideas but also for refining existing concepts.

By remembering the fundamental rule and applying it to product idea formulation, we can see that it is very important to focus entrepreneurial fantasies. Perhaps the most basic ingredient in a software entrepreneurial venture is the initial product offering. This chapter is designed to enhance the success of that offering by providing techniques to create the best market-ready design. The entrepreneur should not proceed with a product implementation unless he or she uses these product definitional tools.

There are five primary techniques used to define product ideas. These are: brainstorming, user surveys, basic research, "building a better mousetrap," and market studies. No one is used exclusively. The reality of product formulation is that many existing companies do not use all of these techniques. However, most organizations do use forms of these techniques, and they will attest to their usefulness.

5.1.1 Brainstorming

There are several basic brainstorming approaches, and they usually involve a group. Even though you plan to work alone, it is best to utilize the group approach, to have others with whom you can discuss ideas. The group may be the entrepreneur(s) plus friends who are knowledgeable in the product area.

The premise of a successful brainstorming session is that one can best create product ideas in a positive, confidence-generating environment. Therefore, a basic rule must be set for any brainstorming sessions that there will be no negative feedback.

The first step in brainstorming is to lock the group in an isolated environment. Isolated means away from telephone and other distractions and interruptions. Some space is required for hard-copy charts, such as a wall or stands. The participants need not be seated at a table, but the room should be comfortable.

The second step is to set the mood. Some brainstorming advocates believe that the participants should be instructed not to bring anything with them to the session. "Nothing" includes no preconceived ideas or notions. Since normally most people do have preconceived ideas and notions and most people like to be prepared for a meeting, it is desirable to issue a premeeting memo which states:

> We will be spending ____ hours brainstorming product ideas. There will be absolutely no interruptions during this session. The purpose of the meeting will be to discuss product ideas with the emphasis on quantity and not quality. Therefore, please be prepared to suggest several ideas and to refrain from offering any criticism of the ideas of others. However, advance preparation is unnecessary. If you have any questions, please contact me.

The third step is preparation for the meeting by the moderator, usually the principal entrepreneur. Although brainstorming experts consider some of the following suggestions to be heretic, they will help ensure the success of the meeting. The moderator should be prepared to present at least three major ideas to the group. At least one of the ideas should be reasonably farfetched and open to criticism. The reason for this is that the farfetched idea will serve as a model to reinforce the group that there should be no negative input. Additionally, the moderator should arrange to bring in several large flip chart pads with at least one flip chart holder. A good visible flip chart holder and set of pads can be obtained for a minimum investment and will continue to serve the business enterprise. The moderator should also bring marking pens or crayons that will not go through the sheets of the flip chart paper to the next sheet. It is useful to have several colors. The moderator should bring an assortment of masking tape and stick pins so that charts can be placed on the walls of the room without permanent damage. All writing should be on the flip charts, since it is very important to save the materials that are created. Finally, the moderator should consider using a cassette recorder to record the meeting. Some product planners swear by the recordings and listen to them after the meeting to detail what occurred. Others believe that recorders inhibit the process. If the moderator is comfortable about being able to document the proceedings without a tape recorder, then no recording device is required.

The session should be conducted in a free-form manner. The moderator should repeat the reason for the meeting and then state the ground rules of no negative criticism. If a general product area is to be discussed, the moderator should briefly define that area. The session then begins with each member of the group in turn giving product ideas, which are listed. The presentation of these ideas should be in enough detail so that the group understands what idea is being proposed, but not in sufficient detail to write preliminary specifications. There is no magic individual with whom to begin. Just begin. List the idea and the details sufficient to build on that idea. Go around the group one time letting everyone list an idea. Then go around again and again until all ideas are listed. Then ask the group to look at the proposed ideas and see what ideas they in turn spark. Several iterations of this process are usually enough to get a wealth of information.

The moderator should be prepared then to review these ideas, restating them to be certain that the correct context has been communicated. Next the moderator should try to group ideas. At this point, the moderator should try to obtain group consensus regarding several promising ideas. There is no secret way to achieve this short of hard work and constructive dialogue. Finally, the moderator should take several of the major themes and ask those present to work up a two- or three-page concept of what needs to be done to get a preliminary design. This final step creates the environment to carry forth new product ideas and design.

After the session the moderator should prepare a written document which summarizes the ideas presented and outlines the next steps agreed upon. This should be sent to all participants along with a note of thanks for their participation. The reason for this effort is to memorialize the activities as well as invite feedback as to discrepancies and further refinements.

Usually the most difficult part of this process is to keep the group from getting bogged down in why an idea is "bad." That type of analysis should come, but not at this session. If the brainstorming effort is kept positive, it will enhance the productivity.

5.1.2 User Surveys

There is a very large and knowledgeable user community, and this group of individuals is an excellent source for product ideas. *There is no question that a software entrepreneur should look to users for product input.* Very few packages with sufficient user input have ever failed. The reason for this is simply that the user is the buyer. If you can identify and satisfy the needs of a sufficient segment for the user community, you will succeed.

There are several basic ways to utilize the information available from computer users: raw product ideas, idea definition as per suggestions from the user about the raw idea, and product surveys. (Product surveys will be discussed in Section 5.1.3.)

Users are a source of raw ideas. Many software companies make it a point to talk about product opportunities with at least a few users each month. The general questions are simply, "Have you seen any good product ideas lately?" and "What products do you think are needed in the marketplace?" The technique is simple and can be used on strangers as well as friends. The questioning can occur face to face or over the telephone. A sample telephone dialogue is as follows:

ENTREPRENEUR:	Hello, Mr. User, this is Joe Entrepreneur. I'm the founder of CZYZ Incorporated. I'm currently working on a business plan for CZYZ and I would like to ask you a few questions. I'll limit this phone call to only a few minutes.
USER:	Fine, but I'm not sure I'm the right person.
ENTREPRENEUR:	Mr. User, I'm certain that you have looked at software products. Have you seen anything recently that really looks good?
USER:	Well, I have seen a really good system from AACC Corporation. It does absolutely everything I've always wanted. It provides . . . .
ENTREPRENEUR:	That sounds really good. What type of package would you really like, but haven't seen?
USER:	I really would like a system that . . . .
ENTREPRENEUR:	I'm currently working on a (very general, ambiguous description . . .). Does that sound interesting?
USER:	Well, you haven't told me much, but I'd suggest . . . .
ENTREPRENEUR:	I really appreciate your input. I would like to talk to you again after I complete a little more of the design. Can I call you then?
USER:	Sure.
ENTREPRENEUR:	Let me make certain I have your mailing address. Can you give it to me?
USER:	Yes, ...
ENTREPRENEUR:	Thanks for your time. Good-bye, Mr. User.

This short dialogue has accomplished several items. First of all the entrepreneur has identified a product idea the user likes. This may key additional ideas. Second, the entrepreneur has heard of an original idea that the user likes. This information may enable the entrepreneur to create new ideas along this line. Finally, if the entrepreneur has an idea, he has been able to test it on a user. The entrepreneur has likely received input regarding his concept. Finally, the entrepreneur can contact the user at a later time to sell the product. Don't be discouraged if the user is noncommunicative. It has been estimated that only 20 percent of all such surveys are productive, but those usually are invaluable.

Many beginning entrepreneurs wish to keep their product ideas secret. Such an approach may negate the potential success of an idea. If the product idea is truly unique and the entrepreneur feels it is certain of quick success, then some secrecy may be justified. If you request that the user not disclose your conversation, he or she will likely agree. If you are really concerned, then choose your users from a set of known individuals whom you can trust. Of course, it may be possible to get users to sign nondisclosure letters, but such an effort may not be justified. Most software firms never require a user to sign a nondisclosure document unless the owner of the product required this. There is no published evidence of a major breakthrough being preempted because of this approach. As the idea becomes formalized, however, the need for protective measures increases. We'll consider such measures later.

5.1.3 Research

In order to develop product ideas, the software entrepreneur should determine the availability of similar or competitive products. There are numerous directories published for all types of software. Some of the more common sources are Datapro, Auerbac, and ICP. Also, computer magazines and newsletters discuss product offerings. Additionally, if the entrepreneur is gearing the product toward a specific manufacturer, that manufacturer's sales literature and product announcements may be helpful.

For each product, the entrepreneur should prepare a data sheet which includes the information listed in Figure 5.1.

The software entrepreneur should also maintain records for all competitive products. Most vendors are more than willing to give out general product information. Obviously the entrepreneur should not under any circumstances be dishonest with respect to requests and certainly should not obtain proprietary materials (documents designated as proprietary, confidential material, or trade secrets). Additionally, many user sites maintain detailed libraries of marketing literature. Information is available from these user libraries and the entrepreneur should obtain such information.

The reason for this type of research can best be illustrated by the following true example. A group of software entrepreneurs chose to develop a comprehensive operations information system for large data centers. The system was to maintain inventory, budget, and reliability information. The entrepreneurs had done the basic research and were proceeding to arrange for sponsor sites. The same week that they planned to begin testing their system, IBM announced a competitive product to license at a very nominal fee. The consequences of this announcement could have been disastrous. However, the group was able to change their plans and bring out a much more ad-

I.   Product, general
    A.   Owning company
        1.   Address
        2.   Telephone
        3.   Contact names
        4.   Other company information
    B.   Sales organization
        1.   Number of offices, salespeople
        2.   Overseas agents
II. Product, specific
    A.   Description
        1.   Features, benefits
        2.   Output records
    B.   Technical details
        1.   Programming language
        2.   Special requirements
        3.   Operating environment
    C.   Pricing information
        1.   Rental and lease plans
        2.   License terms
        3.   Maintenance costs
III. Product track record
    A.   Number of sales
    B.   User names
    C.   Number of releases

FIGURE 5.1   Product information sheet

vanced version of the system which was very competitive. If the group had not been aware of the product announcement, they would have invested thousands of dollars in a marginally competitive product.

The entrepreneur must maintain a very active, continuing research program to determine what products are available. The results of the research must be applied to the final product efforts.

5.1.4   Building a Better Mousetrap

There is a well-known maxim among computer users that pioneers are often those who bear the scars of the battle. Many developers and software companies have begun to realize that there is a very good marketplace for the second or third entry into the market. The reason is simply that the introduction of a new product idea often requires substantial investment in research, development, and user education. In some cases this last factor is very extensive. There is a very good market available to the software entrepreneur who is willing to take an existing product idea and implement it in a superior way. Several companies have been very successful offering better software products than those offered by the computer hardware manufacturer. Additionally, many organizations may look at an existing user implementation and then proceed to develop a user-independent implementation.

This concept may not, on the surface, seem exceptionally attractive to many beginning entrepreneurs. There are, however, numerous justifications for this concept:

1. Most software products exist in one form or another already. What really makes the difference is the design and the implementation.
2. Very few successful software products dominate the marketplace. (There are a few exceptions but they are, in fact, exceptions.) Usually, the leader has captured 20 to 25 percent of the possible market followed by one or two other offerings with 15 to 20 percent each of the potential.
3. There is a proven replacement market for software offered by the hardware vendor. Yes, it is difficult to defeat IBM, but there are many profitable niches left.
4. The users actually want a choice and frequently like to do business with the underdog, or prefer to use newer technology.

The result of these efforts is that many very successful software entrepreneurs study the new offerings from major companies and offer a much better version of those products. The morality of such a venture is easily justified. The legality is proper when no violation of intellectual property laws occurs. There is a very prosperous market available for the truly creative software entrepreneur who can look at existing products and determine that a better implementation can be successful. Yes, there is a market for a better mousetrap.

5.1.5 Market Surveys

There are full graduate-level courses associated with market research. This subsection is a synopsis of several techniques. It is not all inclusive and the reader is urged to read available texts. A corollary of our fundamental rule is that

EFFORT IN PRODUCT DEVELOPMENT SHOULD BE MINIMIZED UNTIL SUFFICIENT MARKET SURVEYS ARE COMPLETED.

The reason for this is that market research is an absolutely fundamental input to product design and review. It should be pointed out that a market survey does not automatically determine the attributes of a successful product. It simply provides input as to customer attitudes and beliefs which will affect the acceptance of a product.

Before beginning any market research, the entrepreneur should identify the goals of the survey. Normally the principal goal is simply to determine the general acceptability of the product concept. Additionally, the various *possible* features of the system should be explored to determine the questions to be asked. The researcher must also decide if further contact will be needed.

In some situations, the entrepreneur may wish to review the prepared format prior to initiation of a detailed survey. The sample size, that is, the number of surveys to be made, is a highly technical and detailed question. In essence, the size of a *random* sample is a function of favorable responses, unfavorable responses, and acceptable error. In general, most researchers in the computer industry tend to ignore these formulae and choose a personally comfortable number of samples. The detailed statistical and mathematical formulae are beyond this discussion, and the more statistically inclined software entrepreneurs are urged to review the reference following this chapter.

Most current software firms consider a sample of 100 large-scale computer users reasonable. In the case of microcomputer programs, for example, organizations may use larger sample sizes since the sample size usually increases as a function of larger potential user population.

What is correct? Obviously, to a certain limit the larger the sample the better. The real key is whether there is a significant enough marketplace to provide for product decision.

Many market researchers believe that it is very important to spend time and effort in the preparation of a questionnaire. There are numerous formats. In general, it is best to begin by easing the interviewee into the process. The initial questions should be easy to answer. Normally they are environmental in nature. For example, it may be important to know what type of computer is used, how many programmers use the computer, what peripherals are available, and so on. Next the questions should lead into the product concept. For example: "Have you ever considered installing a text-editing microcomputer? If so, where did you find your source of programs?" Be certain to include questions that help determine both current and future environments, as well as current and future needs. Finally, the questionnaire should wind down by hitting the key question, that is, are you a prospect in several different ways:

1. Would you purchase such a system?
2. Would you like to serve as a sponsor site?
3. Would you like to receive additional information?
4. Is our product competitive?
5. Do you have money budgeted for this type of product?
6. Would you be interested in such a product?

There should be a clear thank you with the questionnaire. Most software researchers agree that in a mail survey there should be a return envelope.

Normally in a mail questionnaire, the questions are very structured. In order to prepare the questions, the entrepreneur should ask for each question:

1. Will the interviewee understand how this applies to his environment?
2. Will each interviewee interpret the questions the same way?

3. Are there any double negative questions?
4. Is it clear what type of response is called for?
5. Is the question too wordy?
6. Is the question a simple one?
7. Should I cross-check this question (that is should I ask the question a second time a second way)?

There are three basic ways to conduct a survey: in person, by telephone, and by mail. Many surveyors use all three techniques. Normally, in-person interviews prior to telephone and mailings enable the entrepreneur to refine the questions.

Usually, using in-person interviews exclusively is prohibitive. However, several in-person interviews are essential in order to validate the types of answers received by other methods.

Many organizations use telephone interviews. The reason for this approach is that a higher proportion of respondents will agree to a brief telephone survey whereas they may not agree to respond to a mail survey. If a telephone survey is used, the interviewer should quickly introduce himself and the purpose of the interview. There is no rule of thumb as to length of the interview, although interviews should generally be limited to ten minutes or less. If the person being interviewed is truly interested in the subject, he or she may be willing to continue beyond the time limit. The individuals should be given an opportunity to expand on their answers. However, be certain to get specific answers to questions being asked.

Mail surveys should always contain a brief personalized letter introducing the interviewer and usually suggesting the value of the answer. The questionnaires should be printed or copied on quality bond with a clearly laid out format including sufficient space to answer questions. Some organizations utilize premiums or gifts although this is not necessary. Most researchers do include a postage-paid response envelope, as much as a courtesy as an incentive. Both the questionnaire and the response should be preidentified as to interviewee either by code or by an affixed label. Some surveyors remail or personally contact nonrespondents to increase the rate of response.

Any market survey should be reviewed in detail. Normally a master chart is made listing by question each respondent's answers. The entrepreneur should take the time to prepare a written report detailing the response and the findings.

The report should not be biased. Prepare it in such a manner that a disinterested third party can determine positive and negative results. Each positive conclusion, as well as the supporting reasons, should be stated. Each negative reason should likewise be identified, and in a separate section actions with respect to these ideas should be prepared.

Finally, it is a good idea to send a brief separate thank you note to respondents. They have taken the time to respond and obviously may represent future customers.

In Judy Smith's case, she must determine the acceptability of her personnel system. One of the first issues she would face is to decide whom she should survey. She should be interested in the opinions of several groups of people. Certainly data-processing applications managers have defined needs and requirements. Most likely, personnel department managers also know what they desire. In some cases, systems users and experienced analysts also have needs.

Judy would begin by setting up a list of people to be contacted. She could then prepare a questionnaire which begins with some easy initial questions including current procedures, users of the current procedure, programming languages, and computer environment. Next she would begin to question the overall need for a personnel system. Then she would ask specific questions as to her proposed features. Finally she should try to determine if the interviewee qualified as future sales potential.

The data that Judy obtains is very important to the final definition of her product. Not only will it verify the usefulness of her system, it will also supply her with ideas for enhancements. Judy will likely use other techniques to verify her product design. However, this survey will be a very important ingredient.

5.2   MEMORIALIZATION

All techniques that generate product ideas are valuable. Their value is enhanced by maintaining of records.

Most software developers agree that the most difficult aspect of product development is documentation. Most experienced software entrepreneurs attempt to minimize this problem with a continuous memorialization process. This self-documenting approach does not provide final user documentation. However, by developing memorialization documents, the entrepreneur can greatly reduce the final effort for product market readiness.

Most developers prefer to use a large (2- or 3-inch) three-ring notebook with an entire section devoted to product definition. The basic starting place for documentation efforts are the product investigation concepts discussed earlier in this chapter. Obviously the next step in such memorialization is the development of functional specifications. For that reason we will treat functional specifications as an extension of product investigation.

5.3   FUNCTIONAL SPECIFICATIONS

Probably the most lasting necessary documentation is the functional specifications. The functional specifications become the working document from which evolve the product, detailed documentation, and marketing specifications.

The primary task of functional specifications is to tell a potential user what the system will do. In general, the entrepreneur must create a narrative accompanied by graphic illustrations. The functional specifications must detail:

- Input transactions
- Output reports
- Input and output displays
- Data creation and maintenance
- Processing functions

Probably the most accepted way of detailing a system is to address any computer program as a transaction processing system. The entrepreneurs should describe their system by determining the tasks to be performed and the transactions associated with that system.

For example, assume that the entrepreneur is designing a microcomputer-based checking account processing system. The transactions initially are defined as

1. *Check input*
   records information for each check issued
2. *Deposit input*
   records information for each deposit made
3. *Balance inquiry*
   displays checking account balance
4. *Account reconciliation*
   enters in data from a bank statement to reconcile the monthly transactions
5. *Memo posting*
   allows user to create memos for tax and other purposes

For each of these transactions, the developer would determine the modes of input and output. If the input was to be via a CRT display, the rough screen format would be drawn accompanied by explanatory verbiage. If the transaction created an output via a CRT, both the screen format and narrative would be provided. If there are hard-copy reports, the basic report layouts would be drawn with an explanation of contents and uses. Finally, if input forms are used, they would be visually described.

Along with the transaction-oriented information, the developer should provide a one-page overview of what the system should do.

At some point the design must be fixed. However, initially these documents should be part of a feedback loop wherein the functional specifications are reviewed by the designer as well as by sponsor sites, if any. The normal iterative process involves at least one or two reviews. At some monumental time the initial design should be frozen and the entrepreneur must enter into a contract with him or herself, agreeing not to change the functional design unless (a) the product will not work as designed, or (b) the product has little value as designed.

Obviously these two conditions should be tested before the functional specifications are frozen. However, one of the major causes of failure for software projects is the developer's desire to enhance the product before it is done. This usually causes a delay in the completion as well as inviting coding and logic errors.

There is one way to ensure the sanctity of the functional specifications, and that is to have a separate portion of the functional specifications describing an enhancement plan. The enhancement plan is really a set of functional specifications for future versions of the product. The developer may continue to add changes to this enhancement plan.

With the functional specification-enhancement plan approach in mind, the entrepreneur should utilize a chosen set of the five product formulation techniques (brainstorming, user surveys, research, building a better mousetrap, and market surveys) to refine the functional specifications. With a frozen set of design functional specifications and a viable and dynamic set of enhancements, the entrepreneur is now able to proceed with product development.

REVIEW

1. Be certain you understand the five primary techniques by applying them to Joe Brown's structural analysis package. How would he use each?

2. Try self-brainstorming with your product idea by role-playing moderator and participants.

3. Line up some participants for a brainstorming session and conduct one.

4. If you aren't familiar with product review materials, go to the local library and review these materials.

5. Find at least one competitive product for your product idea. If you can't, you had better begin more intense analysis.

6. Take one of the three case examples and determine a better way to prepare the package.

7. Review your product idea and structure your market survey.

8. Prepare your functional specifications prior to any market research. After using the primary techniques, redo the functional specifications.

REFERENCE

1. Chase, Cochrane and Kenneth L. Barasch, *Marketing Problem Solver,* Radnor, Penn., Chilton Book Company, 1977. This is a broad based introduction to practical marketing techniques. It is well worth an entrepreneur's time to review this material.

Chapter 6

SYSTEM SPECIFICATIONS
Now That You Know What You
Would Like to Do, What Will You
Really Do?

6.1 PROJECT PLANS

If you haven't discovered yet that this book strongly encourages planning, we'll further emphasize this methodology by devoting a chapter to project planning and system specifications.

There are literally hundreds of project planning techniques varying from very simple procedures utilizing hand-created charts to very sophisticated computerized project planning methodologies. All of these planning techniques are valid and useful. In general, the best technique for an individual or group is one that:

1. Provides needed information
2. Is easily maintained
3. Is usable by the project team

What information does the software entrepreneur need to manage a project? First of all, the developer/planner must prepare the functional definitions suggested in Chapter 5. The screen, print, and forms specifications are very much a part of the planning process. They must be sufficient to describe the project. Additionally, major components of the system must be identified. These components must be divided into subcomponents, which in turn can become the basis for estimates associated with the plan. Additionally, the project planner must have some concept of resources available. Resources include, but are not limited to, computer time, programmers, documentors, and the like. The source of the information should include not only the developer/planner, but also any implementors who are currently identified. The reason for this is that the information collection phase is very much like a contract negotiation with the participants agreeing on what is to be done and in what manner it will be done. Any experienced planner will emphasize that the plan must be "bought off by the participants."

The planning process works through the capturing and reporting of the primary status information as well as basic changes. Additional functions are associated with the maintenance process. These include preparation and analysis of new schedules and plans based on revised information.

6.2 PROJECT PLANS—PRODUCT IMPLEMENTATION PLANNING

A successful planning system is *used* by the project team. This is the most important attribute and it is tied into the concept of a contract between the planner and the plannees. Project plans that exist solely as an exercise or because of policy are often more disruptive than helpful. Many projects have failed because the project team has rebelled against meaningless controls. In these cases the problem is not always obvious. Perhaps the first question that a manager should ask when a project consistently is delayed is whether or not the project team is sold on the use of a project control system. This sales job is essential since the key to planning is that the planners and the "plannees" must be comfortable with the system and willing to use it for normal decision making. Normally if you are comfortable with your own planning system and feel it is useful, then you should not change it unless you believe a new system provides some benefits. The obvious exception to this is that you may be in an environment that requires its own planning methodology. You should learn to adhere to that methodology. For example, if your investors require monthly status reporting, it might be useful to incorporate those reports into your methodology.

The following is a possible planning methodology. For lack of better terminology it is called a Product Implementation Planning system. Since this book is oriented toward software product development, the emphasis is on a product deliverable.

The prime concept with Product Implementation Planning is that the end or desired outcome of a project is a product. That product consists of many items and not just the set of programs.

We shall expand the definition of the product as we become more market aware. Out initial definition of a product begins with:

1. The functional specifications
2. The system specifications
3. The detailed specifications

4. The programs

5. The documentation

6. A test plan

7. The packaging

Each of these is a set of deliverables. Each deliverable has a set of components. Components of one deliverable are often related to components of another deliverable. The emphasis is on the entire set of deliverables, that is, the product, because the *total* effort of the developer has a *value* which is a direct *function* of the *product*. Therefore, a plan that does not attempt to maximize the value of the product being prepared is not a very good plan for a software entrepreneur.

The first step in Product Implementation Planning is to expand the functional specifications to system specifications and then to utilize these and the deliverable specifications to list the tasks that need to be completed. Let's consider as a product a computer program that performs a basic salesperson expense accounting function by recording transactions, preparing weekly expense reports, reconciling payments, and setting up a brief set of tax-related logs. The principal screens would be those shown in Figure 6.1.

There are five basic transactions, all of which update a common data base producing two types of hard-copy output—an Expense Report and a Tax Category.

Next we would expand these functional specifications to include an initial concept of the data structure and the way each transaction relates to (a) the data and (b) other transactions. Although we will not provide such a level of detail in our example, the

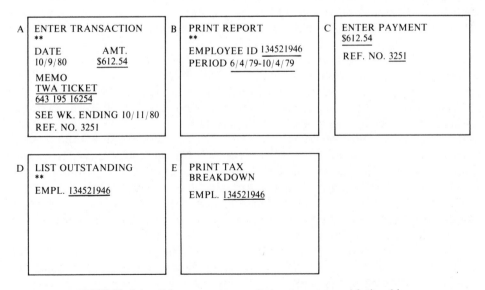

FIGURE 6.1   Salesperson accounting system screen relationships

system specifications should be sufficient for a good programmer analyst to prepare detailed specifications on which the coding is based.

The tasks associated with the program are:

1. Develop screen format processing
2. Develop D/B update for A and C
3. Develop D/B reference for B, D, E
4. Develop print programs for B and E

The remaining product (in a simplified version) requires:

5. Screen definitions
6. Data structure dictionary
7. Print
8. Logic diagrams
9. User documentation
10. Internal documents
11. Test plan

6.3   PERT

We have now listed basic elements that must be done. We will use a simplified PERT technique (Program Evaluation and Review Technique). PERT was originally developed to plan large military projects and has since been adapted to many project control situations.

With PERT, one first lists the tasks and next determines in what order things must be done. For each task, an estimate of time is required. A PERT chart is used to show the tasks in sequence. In our example, assume Figure 6.2 is the PERT chart.

The software entrepreneur may be working alone and thus may have to revise the estimates to reflect this fact (that is that the time shown is elapsed time for each task as if that task were all the entrepreneur were doing. The new estimates show some form of concurrency.) This new chart is shown in Figure 6.3. The darkened areas, referred to as the *critical path,* represent the longest (timewise) path of the effort. In this case, one can determine that the time required to complete this project is 70 days (5 + 5 + 25 + 15 + 20). In general, one would put greater emphasis on schedule adherence for the critical path items, thus trying to meet the *critical* elements of the schedule. The other paths are referred to as *slack paths.*

If the 70-day schedule is unacceptable, the entrepreneur may wish to shorten critical path elements. In our example, screen operations are very time-consuming. This may lead the entrepreneur to consider using a specialized screen development programming aid (likely at a cost). The cost of this aid needs to be analyzed from a

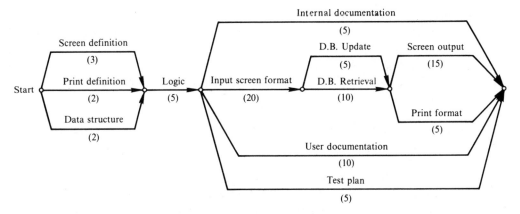

FIGURE 6.2 PERT chart

cost/benefit standpoint. If it saves 15 days and the entrepreneur believes his time to be worth $300 per day, then any cost less than $4,500 is theoretically justifiable. Obviously, other considerations such as an earlier market entry, code and design quality, and distribution rights should influence the decision.

As the project progresses, the chart should be revised to reflect not only completed tasks and their completion date, but changes in estimates and new project schedules.

Obviously, the scope of the project is more complex than our PERT diagrams indicate. A true implementation of Product Implementation Planning would be broken down into many more discrete segments. However, the techniques described are very useful and they do meet our three criteria:

1. *Providing needed information*

   Here, the combination of deliverable definitions and PERT charts very graphically describes the project.

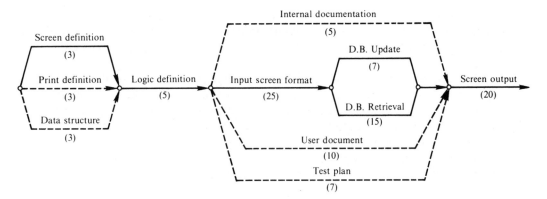

FIGURE 6.3 PERT chart—revised

2. *Being easily maintained*
   The necessary input, including changes, revisions, and updates, is very straightforward.
3. *Being usable by the project team*
   The PERT summary chart as it is initially developed and updated is very usable.

Again, realize that many project planning techniques exist. If you are already familiar with a valid system, you should continue to use it. If not, the Product Implementation Planning technique is very useful.

So far we have limited our discussion to the use of a project plan for a single product. Obviously as the company grows the entrepreneur will continue to utilize project plans for more than one product as well as for maintenance activities. We will not dwell on this other than to state that future benefits to the entrepreneur can be maximized by beginning the first day to develop and use project plans.

Such planning could also be used for evaluations of employee performance. Without discernible goals, employees have a very difficult time achieving excellence. By having the employees participate in this planning process, the entrepreneur can effectively create a contract between the employees and the company.

6.4 SYSTEM SPECIFICATIONS

We have already mentioned system specifications. Rather than emphasize technical programming methodologies, we will instead discuss the market-oriented uses of materials. We can best discuss system specifications by considering what a potential user wants to know.

Someone who is evaluating a software product wants knowledge at various levels. The first question is what the system does and the last question is how the system does it.

Many developers choose to provide two types of documentation, internals and externals. The difficulty with this differentiation is that the externals may not be sufficient to provide a planner or potential customer with sufficient detail to understand the system.

The entry point for the analysis of the differentiation is usually a set of functional specifications which, as we shall see, will serve an important role in the sales aspects of an entrepreneurial venture. These functional specifications do not usually suffice to answer the "how" question. In fact, they usually only whet the appetite of the would-be user without completely answering what the system does.

Normally, after reviewing system specifications the user wants to know more about what the system does. Questions often get to several key areas:

1. What happens if I enter "XXXX" on the CRT screen?
2. Can I add a new transaction?

3. Can I change or add a report?
4. Can I inquire using a different key?
5. Can I search the data base to find "ZZZ"?
6. What hardware system features do I need?
7. Can I add the following new data?
8. Can I print on my forms?

These types of questions quickly require some explanations of how things are done—for example, how the data base is structured; how the CRT screens interface with the applications; and how user exits are provided.

By default, we then construct a definition of system specifications as a set of documents which specify the functions of the system and how they operate. Normally this is presented in a manner analogous to the implementation of the final system, describing modules and data structures in sufficient detail to understand how the system operates.

This type of detail is useful for more than implementation and marketing. It is also necessary for any type of detailed planning activities. For that reason the system specifications are discussed as adjunct to the planning process. However, in no way is this meant to minimize the importance of either of these processes.

REVIEW

1. What are the three reasons for using project control methodologies?

2. This chapter did not really suggest a detailed project control update procedure. Can you structure one?

3. What are your objections to project control?

4. Discuss project control with programmers. How do they react?

5. Make a pact with yourself that you will sell your programmers on project control techniques before they begin work.

6. Set up a PIP routine for your project. In particular, did the PERT chart offer you any surprises?

7. Review current literature to see how others plan software projects.

8. Determine what should be included in the system specifications.

9. Where do functional specifications end and system specifications begin?

10. Where do system specifications end and internal documentation begin?

11. Remember that the only individuals more optimistic than programmers are entrepreneurial programmers. Do you really believe you can make your schedule?

12. Reconsider your estimates to consider the effective person days versus estimated person days. How much time will be devoted to other tasks?

REFERENCES

1. Moder, Joseph J., and Cecil R. Phillips, *Project Management with CPM and PERT.* New York: Van Nostrand Reinhold Company, 1970. This is a very detailed book which includes additional information regarding optimization and computer programs.

2. Robertson, D. C., *Project Planning and Control.* London: Heywood Books, 1967. This is a good introduction to project control concepts.

Chapter 7

IMPLEMENTATION
Doing It

7.1 INTRODUCTION

Once the functional design and initial planning are complete, the software entrepreneur must begin the implementation of the product. The major concerns during this effort are facilities, style, documentation, and project control. Rather than approach this topic from a technical standpoint (an approach that is emphasized in many computer science texts), we will emphasize the business considerations of an implementation of a computer software system.

Implementation is very important. It is hoped that the would-be software entrepreneur is very familiar with the required techniques. In case you need to review those techniques, the Reference section at the end of this chapter lists one of the better texts on this subject.

7.2 FACILITIES

One important decision is on which computer and on whose computer the product will be implemented. These are two separate questions; however, they are related and can be discussed simultaneously. The first consideration can often be answered by identifying the end product marketplace. If the system is designed to run on a specific hardware system, there is a fundamental rule that the development system should replicate as much as possible the end system. There are obvious reasons for this, not the least of which is a hoped-for ease of transformation, without the inevitable minor changes at a user site. Today, however, there is a growing use of special program development hardware systems. These systems are usually geared strictly to the program development task, offering improved response times over those of normal systems and featuring development aids such as language syntax checks and structured design/programing-oriented tools. In many cases the economies of such facilities far outweigh the final tuning and installation cost on another hardware set. Either approach is acceptable. The major requirement is that if a development system is utilized, actual planning for this adaptation must occur. There are, of course, numerous issues that must be considered. These include:

1. Do the programs rely on specific hardware features?
2. Do the programs require special peripherals?
3. Is the native mode environment (operating system) standard?
4. Is the systems mode environment (teleprocessing or data-base system) standard?
5. Are the programming languages required to operate the product available?
6. Will the performance of the product be adversely affected by certain hardware configurations?

There are additional relevant questions uniquely based on the specific product. The software entrepreneur should list these questions and review them, ascertaining the impact of each and planning the final environment.

The second consideration, that of whose computer should be used, is slightly more complex in that it is a function of availability, money, and legal concerns. One major reason for the failure of software entrepreneurs to achieve their schedules is the lack of availability of a test system. This is perhaps the number one passive-aggressive excuse used by programmers and managers. The lesson from this is simply that the environment chosen should maximize availability. There are normally three possible sources for computer development:

1. Purchased computers or computer time
2. Bartered computer time
3. "Borrowed" computer time

Let's deal with "borrowed" computer time first. Many programmers have been tempted to use their employer's computer for development activities without the employer's knowledge or permission. There are at least three reasons that this should not be done. The first is that morally it is incorrect. It may create ill will at a later date when the budding software entrepreneur needs the ex-employer reference. The adage of not burning bridges is very appropriate to the computer software business. The same manager for whom you may have an intense dislike as an employee may turn out to be the one prospect who can be the difference between a profitable and an unprofitable month.

The second reason is the *potential* criminal nature of the act. New laws are being passed which make it a crime if one unlawfully accesses a computer system. The last thing that a software entrepreneur needs during the building of a business enterprise is to be faced with a criminal indictment. Obviously you might "win," but it just is not worth it.

Third, and perhaps most importantly, it is highly likely that if an employee creates a product on his or her employer's computer system, the employer may have a reasonable claim of ownership. We will spend some time in this book discussing the concepts of ownership of software. At this time it is sufficient to note that the more the possibility exists that someone can claim an ownership interest in your software product, the greater the possibility that the value of that product is decreased.

What can an employee do to utilize his or her employer's computer while avoiding these problems? The answer is to obtain a very clear written consent from the employer. This consent should state at least:

1. The employer grants permission to use the computer in exchange for some consideration (perhaps future use of the software package).
2. Such development is beyond the scope of the employee's employment (that is, the employee is not being employed to design this system).
3. The employer releases all claim of ownership in the employee's product.
4. Both employer and employee will mutually hold the other harmless against claims relating to their individual actions.

Since the law governing these activities varies from one state to another and since the actual law changes over time, the software entrepreneur must consult with a knowledgeable attorney to have the consent document drafted.

We have assumed that the employer is willing to grant these rights. Many are not willing to do this, so the developer must consider the remaining two sources—purchase and barter. These two sources are very similar from a legal standpoint. In the case of purchase, the developer is paying to use a system. In the case of barter, the developer is usually trading the package for system use.

The purchase of computer time is probably the cleanest transaction. The entrepreneur must be certain to contractually specify:

1. Costs and billing
2. System availability
3. Unique ownership of the end product
4. Miscellaneous protections such as security and warranties

Most purveyors of computer time and systems have standard agreements from which they are usually willing to vary. Be certain that the final agreement clearly provides that the purveyor has no ownership interest in the final product. Any other clauses are really a function of your negotiating skills. Since this purchase can represent a considerable expenditure, it is a good idea to have your attorney and accountant review the final document.

If one is developing software for large-scale environments such as a large IBM computer, the development system will probably be beyond the purchase capabilities of most start-up software entrepreneurs. The more complex the development environment, the more difficult it will be to find a vendor. There is no unique source of programming development resources. One reasonable method is to begin discussions with computer manufacturers. They may sell time and certainly may be aware of the location of development hardware. Another possibility is to review computer publications. Additionally, most telephone yellow page directories list resources. Unless time is of the essence, the software entrepreneur should talk with several groups. The entrepreneur should list important factors including:

1. *Cost.* This analysis should include a review of type of activity (batch versus online), time of usage (day versus evening), type of service required (normal job submission versus stand-alone), and class of response (immediate versus delayed).

2. *Work space.* Many computer providers furnish minimal work space for development. In most situations, this is only desk space shared with terminals and computer peripherals. However, some computer service bureaus will actually supply private office space. In any case, it's important to look at these facilities and determine if they are sufficient for the developer's needs.

3. *Customer references.* The caveat for doing important business with any organization is to check their references. After you've talked to supplied references, you must then talk with unsupplied references such as users who come into the facilities. Check with friends and associates. You can certainly ask competitors' opinions of your choice. A warning is necessary: giving references is an art cultivated by vendors and furthered by customers who are often unwilling to tell the real story. However, if you're performing a competitive analysis, you can rate vendors relatively.

4. *Programming assistance.* The intelligent software entrepreneur recognizes the need for assistance and is willing to obtain that assistance. Some computer service vendors do have customer support staffs who not only will assist in program setups but will also help the developer solve problems.

5. *System up-time guarantees.* Many vendors will contractually commit to system availability. Computer availability is a very severe and sensitive matter. Aside from bad estimates, the major reason for project delays is the lack of available computer resources. If you can, get a computer service vendor to help indemnify you against losses.

6. *Configuration.* One must examine the hardware and software configuration. Be certain that it is (a) sufficient, and (b) representative. The system must in-

clude necessary software and hardware to do the development. Additionally, the system should be representative of the end-user marketplace.

7. *Service.* There are many providers of computer time. Most are professionals at their trade. Unfortunately, a few are poorly equipped to perform basic tasks such as billing, report deliveries, and personal care. Unless you have unlimited funds, you should insist on prompt billing. Many good service bureaus provide a bill along with each computer run, although naturally there may be additional charges incurred. This is an excellent tool for the software entrepreneur who wants to control costs and avoid monthly anguish at very large bills. Some computer service vendors will place computer output in a common area rather than hold it for request or provide a special box. If you are developing a product, you probably do not want the other users of the computer center to see it. In fact, careless collection and distribution of output may prevent you from protecting the system against piracy.

8. *Personal care.* As in any business relationship, good personal care can be the difference between a satisfactory arrangement and a poor one. Somehow things seem to go a little more smoothly if the computer center staff knows who you are and greets you by name. Look at the service facility when you are evaluating it. Does it seem to be a friendly environment? If so it might be just a little better than its competitor where everyone walks around in an unfriendly manner.

Remember, the entrepreneur must be certain contractually to ensure the unique ownership of the end products. *If the contract does not so state, the entrepreneur must specifically ensure, in writing, that all products developed will remain the sole and exclusive property of the developer.*

If the entrepreneur plans to implement the product of a mini or microcomputer, it may be both feasible and necessary to obtain a system. Even with greatly reduced hardware costs, such an initial expenditure is significant. The entrepreneur clearly should examine the possibility of borrowing a development system from a friendly vendor. Surprisingly enough, some software developers have actually gotten microcomputer manufacturers to underwrite their development costs by not only supplying equipment but also paying a development fee. Remember there is really a software shortage, particularly for microcomputers, so a creative entrepreneur can be very effective. If this borrowing is not possible, some vendors may be willing to rent their systems. Do what you can to minimize cash outlay.

Obviously, the source of computer time is a very important part of the overall plan.

From a legal standpoint, a barter transaction is similar to a purchase transaction. The difference turns out to be one of attitude. Usually because barter is involved rather than cash, both parties evolve a much more carefree attitude. This might be psychologically more comfortable but from a business standpoint it can prove to be a disaster. The barter arrangement usually involves the trading of the package for some amount of computer time. This seems like a simple enough transaction and, in fact, it is. As with most software entrepreneurial transactions, the entrepreneur should review this effort with financial and legal advisors.

The simple barter arrangement may have tax consequences requiring that the computer time received be treated as a cash equivalent (that is, income). There may be only a few ways to structure the transaction to avoid this, but there are many ways to structure the arrangement so as to defer the taxation.

From a legal standpoint, there are two primary concerns. The first is that, as with any business transaction, the entrepreneur should spell out what the agreement is. This prevents future misunderstandings and outlines the obligations of both parties. The second is that the software entrepreneur is trading a very valuable asset, the product. This asset should be protected via a license agreement in a manner similar to a normal sales environment. This prevents unauthorized distribution of the system and clearly states the maintenance and enhancement policies.

To summarize, barter is a very favorable alternative for the computer time required by a software entrepreneur. Proper safeguards should be taken, but with these, the developer may find a cash-free source of computer resources.

7.3 STYLE

A detailed review of "good" programming style is well beyond the scope of this chapter. Rather than discuss the merits of structured programming, GO-TO statements, and other important technical topics, this brief section will look at style as a sales and marketing consideration. The reason for this is that the software entrepreneurs and programmers will likely be unwilling to change their style but may desire to increase the value of their product.

Without a doubt, the major attribute of programs that affects the value of a software package is clean appearance of the code. The words *clean, crisp, elegant, easy-to-read,* and *organized* describe what an intelligent evaluator looks for in source code.

Even if you do not plan to distribute source code, you should be concerned with these factors. Simple techniques such as indentation, comments, recognizable addresses, and subroutine names greatly comfort would-be buyers and tremendously assist future maintainers. Nothing is worse to a programmer than having to maintain someone else's code. If the code is kept clean, a future reviewer will feel much more comfortable.

We mentioned that you might not choose to distribute source code. That choice can be based on several factors. There are two valid reasons for not distributing source code. The first is that the algorithms are exceptionally clever and any exposure might result in loss of competitive advantage. The second is that the maintenance, use, and installation will be easier. There are also two valid reasons for distributing source code. The first is that if you do so, many sales objections are overcome. This is usually more important to the start-up firm, which must overcome the lack of track history. Second, with source code, the users may be able to assist in the maintenance of the system. In either case, from a sales standpoint the buyer should be shown samples of the source and that source should reflect good style.

7.4 DOCUMENTATION

The exact documentation for your package will be, to an extent, a function of the audience for whom it is intended. Usually, a good software product has the following elements of documentation.

1. *Product description.* This serves both as a marketing tool (see later chapters) and an introduction to what the product does. It should describe briefly all input and output screens, all reports, and a synopsis of data-base structure. It should take a feature-benefit approach.

2. *User's guide.* This manual does what the name implies. It tells the users of the system how to use the system. Normally it is a reference manual of control cards and commands. If the system is transaction-driven, there is usually one chapter per transaction. It also details the reports and states how to interpret the data on these reports.

3. *Installation guide.* This document details the methods of system installation and should provide a complete checklist for installation diagnostics.

4. *Internals manual.* If source code is distributed, this document describes the program logic and details the individual modules. If source code is not distributed, this provides details on module exits and interfaces.

5. *Source code (optional).* This must be self-documenting and include comments and module descriptions.

Some software products also include reference cards to assist users. These are very valuable in terminal-oriented systems.

Documentation is a very important ingredient of a successful product. For the most part, users do not believe documentation is adequate. They are often correct. Spending adequate time and energy preparing documentation is very important—and can sometimes be the determining factor in whether a client will select your product.

7.5 PROJECT CONTROL

We have already discussed project control. Any well-run implementation project will utilize a project control mechanism. In the case of multiple implementers, there may be weekly control meetings. These are necessary to bring a product out on time and within budget. Trying to implement a software product without a project control method is like playing Russian roulette with five bullets in the gun. The odds are high that a catastrophe will occur.

———————————————————— **REVIEW** ————————————————————

1. State the factors associated with development site selection.

2. Talk with a few local service bureaus and visit their sites to meet with users.

3. Look at typical programs. Are they readable?

4. Ask a few buyers of software products what they look for in style.

5. List out the documentation for your product. State briefly what will be included.

6. Set up a *written* project control mechanism for your development.

REFERENCE

1. Jensen, Randall W., and Charles C. Tenies, *Software Engineering*. Englewood Cliffs, N.J.: Prentice-Hall, Inc., 1979. This is an excellent detailed text on the software development process. In particular the first five chapters are very well suited as a guideline to the development process. There are also chapters on security and privacy (a topic which we will not dicuss) and on legal aspects of software development. This text is somewhat large-project oriented but the techniques can be applied to smaller ventures.

Chapter 8

TESTING
How to Make It Work for Everyone

8.1 THREE PHASES OF TESTING

Every existing software firm has encountered major product problems which require dramatic and usually destructive activities. Thorough and adequate testing can prevent most of these difficulties. As a general rule, the length of the testing cycle should equal or exceed the length of the programming cycle. In many ways, testing is the most important phase of product development.

There are three phases of the testing process:

1. Implementation testing
2. Product prerelease testing
3. Release and fix testing

These differ in approach but not in objective. The objective of testing is to ensure that the system works. This does not mean that the system works as specified, but rather that *all* operational aspects of the system are successfully implemented. It may be that the specifications for the system are not correct and thus, although the product performs as specified, it does not work. In that case, the specifications must be changed. In reality no system works in an error-free manner. Experienced software buyers recognize this basic fact, so if a vendor is foolish enough to claim error-free operation, the buyer usually begins seriously to doubt that the product is a viable one. A more important claim is that of responsiveness to errors. Therefore it is very important that the developer be able to correct outstanding problems when they occur and to test those corrections to prevent additional errors. Thus, testing really has two objectives: the minimization of errors and the increased ability to respond to errors as they occur.

The three phases mentioned above differ somewhat in approach. For example, implementation testing is really an ongoing effort very much tied into the programming process. Yet prerelease testing is an extension of implementation testing. Both of these flow from each other. The fundamental approach associated with the implementation phase is: "Will the code, as written, run?" In the product prerelease testing, the question is whether the total set of programs that constitute a product run together in artificial *and* real environments. The release and fix testing approach the objective by determining both, "Is the problem solved?" and "With the solution does the system work?" All three can be dealt with by using similar techniques, described below.

8.2   THE IDEALIZED TESTING MODEL

The exact testing procedures differ among software developers and are as much a function of habits (both good and bad) as techniques. This chapter proposes an idealized model useful for all three phases consisting of the following elements:

1. A test plan
2. A test log
3. Quality assurance
4. Product cleanup

After developing this idealized model, we will examine each of the three phases of the testing process.

8.2.1   The Test Plan

The first important component of the Idealized Testing Model is the test plan. This is another area where the use of planning tools is an absolute necessity. A test plan is like a road map in that it provides an excellent reference source for the trip through product testing. It, of course, is not the vehicle for testing nor is it the decision-making process. Competent developers have individualized techniques for solving problems, but experience dictates that a checklist of items to be tested is required.

The test plan is actually more than a planning tool. It is a good vehicle for outlining the features of the system and understanding how the system functions. The very act of preparing the plan prepares one to explain the system in intimate detail. A creative entrepreneur can utilize the test plan as an integral part of marketing documentation.

As we shall see, there are numerous ways to sell the final product. One of these is to license an existing firm, which will in turn sell the product. In this case, most acquirers of software require that the system be thoroughly tested by their organization. Often a well-written test plan can expedite this process and increase the value of the acquisition.

By using a test plan the software entrepreneur improves the chance for delivery of a quality software product, thus also increasing the value of the software. A test plan does increase the profitability of a product offering.

The real heart of the test plan is the achievement of a confidence level in product operation. A test plan must be developed to include at least:

1. The individual elements to be tested, including module-by-module breakdowns of input format required and output expected. Editing functions, arithmetic validation, and data maintenance must be exercised. Additionally, each error code should be tested.
2. A system testing of module interfaces and relationships to validate calling or control sequences as well as processing consistency. Further examination should be made of system operation with missing modules.
3. Some type of "trace" or sampling methodology to ensure that code paths are used and that unnecessary looping does not occur. Such tracing may require special tools or newly written code.
4. Documentation verification by testing sample control cards, transactions, and generation options in order to be certain that they work in the manner specified.
5. A test data system to be used with predetermined "successful" results. This can provide much (but not all) of the confidence required.

A test plan guides the developer through the test process. An important adjunct to that process is the maintenance of a test log.

8.2.2 The Test Log

Like any set of important events, the testing process is not only planned but also memorialized. Records should be maintained stating, for each computer run, the results including both successful achievements and failures. This is a test log and it serves two valuable purposes. The first is that the software entrepreneur can specifically maintain a detailed record of progress and assess this progress against plans. Second, the test log will serve as a basis for further error solution and product support in that it establishes certain problem trends and can be cross-referenced by symptom to direct the support personnel to the likely areas of the actual difficulty.

As a rule of thumb a major product development should blow up at least once during the testing cycle. If it does not, the software entrepreneur probably is not sufficiently exercising the system. By reviewing the test log prior to release, the developer can gain confidence in the reliability of the system. Obviously error-prone modules can be examined in greater detail prior to system release. The history of testing can be quite useful when enhancements and improvements are conceived.

As we shall see when we begin to review product support, the test log serves as an excellent reference guide for future support. This greatly enhances the responsiveness of the developer to problems.

Many software developers remove some portion of the computer printout run-time information and note the results of the test. The test log continues to be a living document. It is used during the quality assurance process and is normally maintained throughout the life of the software process.

The test log coupled with the test plan can also be utilized as a back-up sales support tool. A well-done test plan and test log may sway a cautious prospect who is concerned about reliability.

8.2.3   Quality Assurance

Later in this chapter we will examine various quality assurance functions in detail. This subsection will serve as a basic introduction to that function.

Most established software firms have separate development and support groups. For psychological (ego) reasons, the development group is usually a higher-status organization while the maintenance group is considered as lower-status positions. The cold, hard fact is that the profitability of a software company is often directly proportional to the success of software maintenance.

The normal methodology is that the product is developed and then some form of sign-off occurs which then makes the product the responsibility of the maintenance/support group. Sometimes the development group signs off, in some cases the support group signs off, and in a growing number of cases there exists a quality assurance group to "accept" the product. This quality assurance function reviews the test plan and the test log and usually performs its own testing to be certain a quality release is present. There are obvious conflicts between an aggressive sales force which needed the product yesterday, a development group which believes in their product's perfection, and a quality assurance function. A software entrepreneur may have to serve individually as all of these groups. However, it is important to isolate the tasks.

Before the product is released, the developer must review the tests and go several steps further. Even if the initial customers agree to be pioneers, the developer must recognize that he or she may have only one chance in the marketplace. One really "bad" installation usually outweighs a dozen good ones. The code should be clean, the product should work, and, of course, the product should be revised to reflect the changes brought about by testing.

The quality assurance function not only is concerned with product release but should also be concerned with *actual* product quality. This means that not only does the quality assurance group theoretically sign off on product release, it must also audit the system quality as it is perceived by users. We will discuss the maintenance function in a later chapter.

8.2.4 Product Cleanup

Take any existing software product and review the documentation and code. You can safely bet that inconsistencies exist.

The purpose of the product cleanup phase is to minimize these inconsistencies. By using the test log as a guide and following with the documentation developed by the product support function, the software entrepreneur can greatly improve the cleanliness of a product offering.

Changes made during development, testing, and enhancements should be reflected in all documentation including manuals, program comments, and operating procedures. If the documentation has not been changed after testing, the entrepreneur had better lock himself in a room for a week to see why not. Changes are a necessary fact of life and should be made prior to release to the public. Changes are ongoing and many entrepreneurs establish a change control mechanism.

8.3. ORGANIZATIONAL STRUCTURE

We have introduced the thought that the responsible parties for system testing vary with different firms. Many software firms have a group either totally or partially devoted to product testing. If a quality control group exists only to serve exclusively as the final word for product release, it normally can prepare a detailed test plan, a testing exercise, and an analysis of the results. Unfortunately, this is not usually a prestige group and the experience of the people associated with this effort is usually lower than desirable, often causing the quality control function to become a paper tiger. In other organizations, the reliability function may be part of a larger organization which is responsible for product distribution or customer support. Usually the same stigma is associated with the quality control function, even as a part of larger organizations.

Regardless of the organizational structure, some form of quality control must exist and this effort should utilize the idealized model. We will further examine this organizational dilemma when we look at product support. For now we will treat quality control as a management problem and reemphasize its importance.

8.4 USER TESTING

Most test plans include a set of user tests of the product. The major reasons for user testing are that the product may behave differently in user environments and it may be subject to new or increased demands.

In some cases user testing occurs at the same time as nonuser (that is, development) testing. In other cases, it will follow successful nonuser testing. Some companies utilize an initial screening procedure which is less thorough than final field release testing. This latter technique involves several sign-offs and is a more thorough and more difficult procedure.

User testing is normally of two types. The first is an interactive procedure whereby the development team assists in the installation of the system and participates in the testing. The second is a trial-like installation at the user site.

The interactive mode of user testing serves several purposes:

1. The user CPU or operating system may well differ from the development base, thus providing different environmental testing.
2. The user will likely use the system in a real manner, thus providing volume transaction loading unavailable to the development group.
3. The user can exercise the documentation by asking questions which provide corrections to the system.
4. The users can be asked for and assisted in the provision of user stories.
5. The development group can make on-the-spot fixes and corrections, thereby decreasing the repair cycle.

Independent user testing serves several basic user purposes:

1. Simulation of real world usage without interference from the development group.
2. Testing of support mechanisms by requiring remote fixes and consequential documentation.
3. Validating the confidence level in system quality.

The usual process is to treat such independent testing as alpha or beta testing and hope that the user will exercise the product prior to general system release. There should be some formal agreement with the test sites so that they will actually exercise the system and faithfully report errors. Often some form of discount is offered to such test sites.

8.5   RELEASE AND FIX TESTING

Both implementation and prerelease testing are similar in nature and concept. They have a single, ultimate goal, which is to release a quality product. However, testing does not end with product release. With the maintenance function is a continuing obligation to test both fixes and new releases of the product. We will discuss the maintenance function later in this book. At that time, remember the same testing principles and the same generalized model apply.

1. Try to predict the consequences of poor product testing.

2. What are your current implementation testing procedures?

3. This chapter has not dealt with concepts of unit and system testing. If you are familiar with these techniques, how might they be applied? If you are not familiar with these techniques, review existing literature.

4. Prepare a test plan for your product, then review this plan to see what you have left out. Compare it to your product description. Have you tested every feature?

5. How do you plan to set up a quality assurance function? (It's better to consider your strategy now while you have the time rather than later when you're rushed to get out your product.)

6. Can you identify one or two user sites for product testing? If not, how can you cultivate a few friendly sites?

REFERENCE

1. Jensen, Randall W., and Charles C. Tenies, *Software Engineering.* Englewood Cliffs, N.J.: Prentice-Hall, Inc., 1979. This book is an excellent source for technical material.

Chapter 9

MARKETING
How to Position the Product for Fun and Profit

9.1 INTRODUCTION

Many professional computer marketing executives begin any discussion with non-marketing executives by stating, "Of course you realize that when I speak of marketing I am really not talking about sales but rather marketing." Then usually the discussion immediately jumps into a dialogue about the sales program. The reason for this is not the ignorance of the marketing executive, but rather the emphasis on how to sell a product.

What is marketing? It is a detailed analysis of the marketplace and the determination of the requirements to satisfy the needs of the marketplace. It is the function of marketing personnel to determine product requirements and decide how to bring that product to the marketplace. This latter element begins to evolve into a sales plan (the topic of the next chapter). Part of an "acceptable" marketing function is to provide sales tools. As sales occur, or fail to occur, the marketing function is to continue to examine the marketplace and provide feedback as to how the sales plan should be adjusted and what product changes are required. We've already begun to discuss market and product planning. This chapter will emphasize the sales and marketing aspect of the software enterprise with occasional review of some sales fundamentals.

In Chapter 5 we mentioned the marketing skills required to plan a product. Let's take it as a given that the initial product idea has been verified by valid marketing techniques and that the software entrepreneur has followed our guidelines for product development and testing. About sixty days prior to product release the developer/entrepreneur should become a part-time computer software marketing executive.

Let's first look at how the larger software firms structure the marketing function. Most separate marketing from sales and engineering. All three of these functions usually report to upper management (vice-president or director levels). The marketing groups are normally product line oriented. In many cases there is a product line manager with several product managers reporting to him or her. There is no firm number of products for which the product manager is responsible, although this is often a function of work allocation. In some cases there are product specialists working for the product manager. In some organizations the product manager is entirely responsible for the product marketing function. In other cases the product manager is responsible for everything except planning and advertising, although he or she works closely with these other activities.

Given that a large marketing department is beyond the scope of most start-up ventures, we will try to identify exactly what a marketing department does and how an entrepreneur might accomplish its functions.

9.2 PRODUCT PLANNING

We have already begun to examine this area. However, product planning goes far beyond the initial product offering. Once a product is brought to the marketplace, additional releases must be planned to include enhancements, error corrections, and interfaces with newly supported environments.

We will devote most of Chapter 15 to enhancements as a business. Enhancements are a very important marketing consideration since they are what keeps the product viable. In most cases enhancements are dictated by customers, competition, and the developers. Current customers are usually quite happy to suggest new features. Competitive products often force additional enhancements. The developers thrive on providing enhancements. It's the job of the software marketeer to prioritize these sources and add marketing insight.

Most of Chapter 14 is devoted to product support. The marketing aspect of product support is twofold. The product manager must be certain that errors are, in fact, being corrected and the corrections are, in fact, being distributed to the customer base. The product manager must also be certain that cleanup releases of the product are planned so that the ultimate distribution tape does not look like a poorly made patched product. There often exists a very unfortunate attitude of "It isn't my job" among product marketeers. If the product is not maintained, it can't be sold. Thus, maintenance is a very important task for the marketeer.

Regardless of the type of product offering (systems or applications software) or the type of computer (large mainframe, mini, or micro), it is a fact of life that the product must change with changes in the operating environment. These may be in the form of new operating system features, such as new data-management routines, or it may be in the form of new hardware features, such as special CRT formats. The product offering must stay operational in new operating environments and stay current with new features of the operating environments. Thus, the marketeer must be certain that these changes are planned and implemented.

9.3 MARKET ANALYSIS

The good marketeer knows the marketplace and analyzes that marketplace.

In the case of large-scale computers, the marketeer analyzes the breakdowns of the total population to know which subset will be prospective users. For example, the marketeer will most likely know the distribution of operating systems, data-base systems, and computer size. If the product offering requires a special teleprocessing environment such as CICS, the marketeer will know the total number of sites in the U.S. and non-U.S. markets.

For nonturnkey minicomputer offerings, the marketeer will determine who purchases the minis (end users, OEMs, etc.), where they are located, and from whom they are purchased. For turnkey mini systems, the marketeer will normally know how large and where the end user population is. In some cases the marketeer may be more interested in where sales outlets are that cater to that population. (For example, a medical office system might be best sold through medical equipment distributors.)

For nonturnkey microcomputer offerings, the situation is somewhat confused as to distribution media and customer base. Some systems are sold mainly to individuals who already own a micro. Thus the number of installed units is very important. However, many micro users also purchase software from computer stores. Thus the number of such retail outlets is also important. In the case of turnkey micro systems, the basic data required are similar to those required for turnkey mini systems.

Once these data are obtained, they must be analyzed. Of course such analysis is performed for many marketing functions. Initially the analysis consists of sales projections, sales plans, and advertising plans. Eventually it must be expanded to provide competitive analysis and product strategies.

There is no rule of thumb as to how to project sales. There are two basic schools of thought. The first is to look at the marketplace size, examine competitive products, and then estimate a realistic capture rate. This is a valid technique if the sales ability of a firm is not constrained by its distribution channels. The second technique begins by examining the distribution capabilities and estimating sales based on this capacity. The projections are then tested against market size. For large-scale computer systems, most software firms believe that 20 to 35 percent of the total market size is achievable as a function of competition. For nonturnkey mini and micro systems the actual capture rate is usually much smaller because of the specialized nature of the product. For turnkey systems, the capture rate is usually a function of competition, which is an estimated maximum potential based on the total number of competitive offerings and the number of buyers.

We will discuss sales plans in detail in the next chapter. For now it is important to mention that usually an estimate of market potential and the geographic distribution of the users serves as a guide to determining the best approach.

9.4 ADVERTISING PLANS

Market analysis is one factor in developing an advertising plan. There are several important factors of such a plan. The first is *purpose*. There are two primary purposes for advertising—lead generation and image building. Lead generation clearly is designed to create a backlog of prospective customers. Image building is a less tangible purpose, which normally involves establishing an awareness of the company in the minds of the buying public.

A second factor in an advertising plan is *audience*. The choice of advertising placement is often geared to the intended audience. In some cases that group might be computer executives; in other cases it might be applications designers. In still others it might be end users or hobbyists. There is usually some correlation between the magazine or journal and the type of readership. Most media provide advertising kits which detail rates and readership, and such kits are very helpful when one is deciding where to place advertising.

Another major factor is *associated sales programs and campaigns*. An advertisement in conjunction with a seminar series or a mailing campaign is a very effective tool. Many smaller firms do little single-effort advertising but always tie it into other efforts. Usually advertisements are repeated several times for reinforcement.

Another factor is *budgets*. Advertising is not inexpensive. There are usually discounts for multiple placements. In some ways advertising is a chicken and egg analogy: Sales are required to pay for advertising and usually advertising is necessary to generate sales.

An additional factor is the *ad content*. It is advisable for an inexperienced entrepreneur to use professional help in ad preparation. There are three benefits to this. First of all, an agency has experience in ad creation and production. Second, most advertising firms are familiar with media sources and can recommend proper choices. Third, most firms do receive discounts which assist in paying for their effort. Not all advertising firms are experienced in computer software. It is questionable if such experience is required, but it may be helpful.

A final factor is *measurement of success*. For example, if the purpose of the advertisement was to generate leads, the entrepreneur will want to determine how many leads were generated and of what quality they were. If the ad was part of a total campaign, the entrepreneur will want to ask the respondents to the total campaign if they saw the ad. In some cases, the media will survey respondents. This factor is not as simple as it sounds. Most software firms have intuitive beliefs about the results but really cannot provide quantitative measurement.

An advertising plan should contain the following items:

1. A statement of purpose
2. A schedule of ads
3. A description of ads
4. A schedule of concurrent events
5. Measures of success

The advertising plan is normally prepared by product or product time for a fixed period of time (six months or twelve months). The plan should be revised as necessary in order to adjust for changes in market conditions or campaign failures.

Before leaving the area of advertising we should point out that there is a vociferous minority that believes advertising is the most useless promotional tool available for software firms. To date, there are no definitive studies to test that hypothesis, but there is some evidence that advertising that is not tied into a strong sales and promotional campaign is ineffective.

9.5   COMPETITIVE INTELLIGENCE

Many company marketing groups devote one or two individuals solely to gathering industry intelligence. In some cases the product manager is responsible for determining what competitors are doing. In general, competitive analysis provides insight as to other companies' activities and other product offerings.

There are two aspects to reviewing other companies. First, there is a strong direct competitive analysis. Each product line must be analyzed to provide insight as to:

- Who are the competitors?
- What features does their product line offer?
- What pricing strategy do they utilize?
- What is their market share?
- Why do people prefer competitive products?
- Do they have special or unique sales and marketing tactics?

Second, each competitor must be reviewed as to strategy. (Strategy is a long-term policy such as a three-year growth plan or a one-year acquisition schedule.) There are some key sources of such strategies. Customers and prospects may indicate in what direction a competitor is moving. Often trends can be noticed from product decisions. Some market survey organizations provide some intelligence. Employment ads for competitors can supply valuable insight into new product activities. There is also an excellent wealth of competitive analysis that can be gained from lost business reports. (We'll discuss this later in this book.)

Competitive analysis not only is useful for selling marketing policies, it is a necessity for sales training.

9.6 SALES TRAINING

Some larger organizations have special training departments. As we shall see, the training required to keep a sales force in action is very strenuous. Most product managers with successful product lines attribute much of their success to training.

Usually it is a marketing function to prepare sales presentations, to train the salespeople in those presentations, and to provide the salespeople with adequate product knowledge. There is no one way to accomplish all of this. A good start is to develop a product notebook which contains all sales materials, presentations with scripts, competitve product analysis, frequently asked questions with answers, and pricing information. Usually the salesperson will carry this notebook for the first several months. A sales training program can be based on this notebook and geared to the individual needs of the sales group and the product.

Like any form of education, sales training requires reinforcement. Periodic retraining is a good idea. Many product managers also go on joint sales calls with the sales force to provide additional education.

Education must be provided to the sales force regardless of the type of organization. If an actual force exists, personalized training is a necessity. With a distribution channel such as retail stores, judicious use of cassettes or video tapes will be worthwhile. There is usually only one chance to get a prospect interested. Insufficiently educated salespeople can destroy a sale.

―――――――――――――――――― REVIEW ――――――――――――――――――

1. State the difference between sales and marketing.

2. What is a product manager?

3. List all marketing functions that come to mind (in addition to those listed in this chapter).

4. How do you propose to handle product planning?

5. What sources can you find for market analysis?

6. What advertising do you read? What sources are available?

7. What competitors do you foresee and how do you plan to monitor these competitors?

8. How do you plan to train salespeople?

REFERENCES

1. Brannen, William H., *Successful Marketing for Your Small Business*. Englewood Cliffs, N.J.: Prentice-Hall, Inc., 1978. This book is not geared to the software industry; however, it does emphasize many topics of interest such as product, place, price, and promotional strategies.

2. Cafarelli, Eugene J., *Developing New Products and Repositioning Market Brands*. New York: John Wiley & Sons, 1980. This is a good study of many issues of importance to the software entrepreneur as his or her company matures. Again this is not oriented toward computer software so some material may not be relevant.

3. Chase, Cochrane, and Kenneth Barasch, *Marketing Problem Solver*. Radnor, Pa.: Chilton Book Co., 1977. This is a well-written basic marketing text which not only deals with market research but also serves as excellent background for an entire marketing program. Like most marketing texts, this one tends to be nonsoftware oriented.

4. Crow, Edwin L., Frances A. Davis, and Margaret W. Maxfield, *Statistics Manual*. New York: Dover Publications, Inc., 1960. This is an excellent reference for those who wish a more advanced reference document.

Chapter 10

SALES PLANNING
How to Plan a Sales Effort

10.1 INTRODUCTION

In conjunction with a marketing effort, a software entrepreneur must thoroughly plan the sales activities. If the plan is to be dynamic, it requires well-thought-out strategies and tactics. This chapter will deal with the fundamental issues of sales management: how, when, where, and why.

10.2 HOW

One basic issue of software sales is how the entrepreneur plans to sell the product. There is a limited set of possibilities:

1. *By self-selling*. The entrepreneur who wishes to sell his or her own product may do so by in-person sales, telephone, mail order sales, or a combination of techniques.
2. *Through the building of a sales force*. The entrepreneur may wish to hire or associate with experienced salespeople.
3. *Through the use of independent agents*. Recently a reasonably significant group of quality software sales agencies have evolved.

4. *Through the granting of marketing rights to existing software companies.* A large portion of the major software firms look to outside developers to provide software products.

5. *Through publishers or retail manufacturers.* This is very prevalent for mini and microcomputer software organizations.

10.2.1 Self-Selling

Of these techniques, self-selling is the most widely used. This does not mean that it is the best. However, it may be the easiest with which to begin. Believe it or not, anyone can be a salesperson. Several sales training programs emphasize this by showing that if you could train an ape to ask for the order, the ape would be a successful salesman. It is not quite that simple, but self-selling requires only two basic characteristics. The first is goal-driven actions. Probably the major characteristic of successful software salespeople is that they set goals usually on a daily basis and they push themselves to achieve those goals. The goals are often simply to telephone X prospects, to visit with Y potential customers, to deliver Z proposals, or to close N sales. Truly successful software salespeople work long hours and recognize the pipeline theory of sales, which works as follows. If you make unsolicited calls to, say, twelve prospects per week, you can likely arrange to visit six of them, of whom three will be receptive to a proposal and one can likely close. There are delays between each event and a successful salesperson will have a pipeline of 10 to 20 prospects and 5 to 10 proposals. Today a trained software salesperson with a decent product or products can earn compensation in six figures in an average year. This represents the upper 10 percent of the industry, with industry averages probably approaching $40,000 to $50,000 per year. The achievers usually are not more intelligent nor are they much luckier; they just work harder.

The second characteristic required for software sales is persistent closing. Any basic sales course will present an entrepreneur with techniques for closing. Some salespeople ask for an order at every meeting, while others selectively attempt to close. There are benefits to both approaches. What is important is that usually customers do not order a software product without being asked to do so. The key is that many closing techniques are available. The most important aspect of these techniques is how comfortable the salesperson is asking for an order. If you plan personally to sell your product, you should be aggressive and fearless when it comes time to ask for an order.

The software entrepreneur should recognize that the self-selling approach uses up valuable resources including time, money, and psychological energy. To launch a software sales effort, the entrepreneur must spend at least twenty to thirty hours per week, thus straining his or her ability to continue to work on the product. Sales efforts also require money. Telephone costs alone can average $1,000 or more per month with at least that much being spent on travel and office support. Selling is psychologically demanding. The effort often creates emotional roller coasters with waves of pleasure soon replaced by the despair of failure. All salespeople experience this. The better salespeople can cope with this effect. However, there are numerous sales dropouts and the emotional demands are a prime reason.

Even if you choose not to sell the product yourself, you an greatly increase your value to the entrepreneurial process by experiencing the sales process. This is an important growth exercise. However, this growth should not get in the way of a successful product sales program. Thus each entrepreneur must seriously determine if the self-sales approach is right for him. If the entrepreneur begins to sell the product himself, he should be prepared to reevaluate that decision and to find an alternative approach should it not work out as planned. If the decision is to proceed, the entrepreneur should recognize there are varying approaches to selling, as well as combinations of these approaches.. Three common methods are in-person sales calls, mail order, and telephone.

In a normal model for an in-person sales effort, an individual goes through the telephone, visit, proposal, and closing sequence. A creative individual may begin by sending a letter of introduction to a company stating that he or she will call at a certain time. Then a telephone call is made and usually followed by a letter summarizing the discussion and confirming the next action. A meeting or a set of meetings follow at which time the product is presented and questions are answered. This is followed by some form of proposal which may be detailed and formal or as informal as a cover letter with a contract. Then the closing cycle is begun, and, it is hoped, a contract is signed. Of course each of these steps requires follow-up, and time delays are always present.

There are numerous sales courses available, some of which are geared specifically to the computer software industry. If you have never sold before, they may be very useful. Even if you are experienced at sales, they could provide some valuable updates. The telephone company can provide information and training on telephone selling. Usually the best sales training is really on-the-job with self and, if possible, peer review. Don't be embarrassed to rehearse your pitch. Some very good salespeople have never had formal training, but almost all good salespeople read sales-oriented literature and most continue to revise their approaches.

Recently two new additional techniques—mail order sales and telephone sales—have evolved in the software industry, and they are usually intertwined with the older technique of advertising. Some software companies do not have field sales forces, but rather use a combination of mailings, advertising, and telephone sales. This approach doesn't always work well, although it may have some success with less technical, less expensive products. If the product is technical or expensive, usually some form of supplemental support is necessary, such as audiovisual materials, seminars, or self-training devices. There really is little difference in the basic resource requirements of either direct or mail order sales. Both require time and devotion. Both are psychologically demanding. Usually mail order sales require less of a financial commitment, although as the complexity of sales aids increase, the expenses also increase.

There is no one model for mail order selling, but the following can provide some guidance.

The software entrepreneur must first obtain and maintain a mailing list. There are numerous commercial sources available, and the charges for such lists vary a great deal. The best way to evaluate a list prior to using it is to talk with users of the list. Is it current? Does it reach the type of person to whom you wish to sell? Does it provide sufficient information such as CPU type or firm size? There are two ways to purchase such lists. The first is to buy a set of labels which may be affixed to envelopes. The advantages to this are that the cost is usually reasonable and the use of the labels facilitates actual mailing. The disadvantages are that it is for one-time use and that selection of individual accounts may be difficult. The second way to obtain a list is to buy it (with optional renewals) in a booklike form, in a specially prepared form, or for computer media. The advantage to this method is the flexibility associated with the media. The disadvantage is that such a purchase is often costly and requires additional work for a mailing. In either case, the lists are really proprietary to the publisher and may not be copied without explicit approval of the publisher. (Most lists contain "trigger" or dummy names to be certain that the list is not misappropriated.)

The next step is to prepare a mailing. The entrepreneur who can afford a word-processing system is fortunate, because personalized mailings usually receive better attention. Without a word-processing system, he or she can still personalize letters by printing the body on letterhead with the date, address, and greeting personalized. There have been studies showing that personalized letters are more likely to be read, but quite a few very successful mail order software firms do not personalize their materials. Included with the letter is usually an attention-getting product specification sheet. This is normally one sheet (two sides) in order to minimize mail expenses. There is usually a return reply postage card included. Obviously, mailings differ. Some have a gimmick; others are straight. Some are on a small envelope; others are in oversize envelopes. What is important about the content is its impact. If you can do the job with a small piece—fine. If you require a gimmick—fine. Try a few different techniques to see how they work.

The final step is follow-up. For minicomputer software and some less expensive systems, orders may come in directly with the reply. Some mail order firms call each person to whom a mailing is made. This is usually done with personalized mailings. Usually a software firm follows up respondents merely by sending additional information and personally contacting the person requesting information. The mode of operation then is very similar to that of telephone sales which is discussed below.

The cost of mailings is increasing with higher postage and printing costs. Yet with the increasing expense of a sales force, the mailing technique is a valid one, particularly when part of a total sales plan.

Telephone sales are gaining in popularity among software firms. There are several large, successful firms that boast inside their boardrooms that their sales force never sees a client. In fact, several six-figure-a-year software salespeople sometimes send their photographs to clients to let them know who is on the other side of the phone.

Since this is a relatively new approach to software sales, there are no hard and fast rules. However, there do seem to be some consistent factors among the successful firms:

1. Regardless of sales skills, the sales force is well-trained via a script, rehearsals, and so on to pitch the products.
2. Strong administrative support mechanisms assist the salespeople in their job.
3. Extra sales support materials, such as video tapes and newsletters, are available.
4. The phone sales technique is characterized by patience and personality on the part of the sales force.
5. Strong company image building gets immediate recognition from prospects.

A telephone sales force can be successful. The management of such a group is not a small matter, however, and in the long run, support costs may eat into the savings from a nontraveling group.

Most larger software firms now use all of these techniques in one form or another. There is no one right way for a beginning entrepreneur, but all three concepts, sales calls, mail order sales, and telephone sales, should be considered.

10.2.2 Building a Sales Force

A second viable approach to selling is to bring into the business a salesperson or sales manager who will in turn build a sales force. The advantages to this approach are quite obvious. The entrepreneur may devote energies to other parts of the business while the salesperson brings in the sales. This usually results in greater gross and net revenue.

The chief disadvantages to this are as follows:

1. It is costly to bring in a good salesperson and normally will require considerable start-up funding.
2. A key salesperson will usually require an equity position and thereby reduce the entrepreneur's ownership.
3. Salespeople are notoriously difficult to control and often greatly increase the intrapersonal conflict situations.
4. It is becoming exceptionally difficult to build a sales force due to the lack of qualified salespeople and the cost of building a sales force, and thus it is less and less likely that, without major capital infusion, a new company can ever obtain sufficient sales coverage.
5. Without experience, the entrepreneur may not be able to evaluate the applicants.

Many software entrepreneurs have little sales experience and do not know what questions to ask of potential salespeople. Here are some possibilities:

1. Describe how you sell. (See if this type of selling is compatible with your product.)

2. Have you achieved quota? (Discuss this in detail. See if the quota was realistic. Ask for documentation.)

3. What support do you need? (If the salesperson has used many individuals to sell, you might not be able to support him or her.)

4. What accounts have you sold and can I contact them? (The best way to learn about salespeople is to talk with their clients.)

5. How will you build our sales force? (Determine if the person has experience or, lacking that, ideas.)

6. Why are you leaving your current job? (The answer might be "cry-babyish" such as, "They increased my quota" or "They took away my accounts." Be certain that the individual is stable.)

7. Why do you want to work for a start-up company? (You really want an entrepreneurial type. Many ex-Fortune 100 superstars have failed miserably with small companies.)

Access to a competent salesperson is usually beneficial to a start-up company, and the entrepreneur should certainly consider this as a possibility.

10.2.3 Independent Agents

There are a growing number of independent sales representative firms that specialize in local or national representation for software firms. In general, these reps usually have a portfolio of products they sell. Normally the representatives have the customer sign an agreement directly with the developer, although often the developer does not interface with the prospect until after the contract is signed. In most cases, the developer supplies all new releases and maintenance.

The advantages to this approach are:

1. There is usually little if any start-up cost on the part of the representative or the developer.

2. The reps usually are experienced salespeople who do not require detailed sales training.

3. The reps are compensated directly by sales and thus are motivated to sell the product.

4. The reps will often provide product input to the entrepreneur.

The disadvantages are:

1. The compensation is normally higher than to a sales force. The commission normally varies from 15 to 50 percent as a function of price, product completion, and sales cycle.

2. There is normally no direct control mechanism over the rep, so the achievement of sales may not live up to the entrepreneur's expectations.

3. The reps may actually sell several competitive products, decreasing the entrepreneur's achievable market share.

Normally the major difficulty in this approach is finding a rep firm. The entrepreneur usually must consider several sources, including trade publication advertisements, other firms, users, and industry associations. Once a rep is found, the entrepreneur should have a written agreement with the firm describing the arrangement in detail. The entrepreneur should be prepared to live up to this agreement.

10.2.4   Existing Software Firms

Most major software firms look to outside entrepreneurial developers as a source of product development. The normal mode of operation is for the software firm to acquire a product after it has existed for a period of time with a proven track record. As a rule of thumb, the value to a software company is greater when at least ten users exist with a one-year history of use. However, some software companies are beginning to take virgin products. The entrepreneur is well advised to recognize the value of customer reference for this as well as other approaches.

The usual mode of operation is for the software firm to acquire exclusive ownership of a product and give the developing company a combination of cash and royalties, usually resulting in an average royalty of 20 to 35 percent.

The advantages of this approach are:

1. The software company has an existing sales force with an established customer base, thus likely increasing the probability of market penetration.

2. Usually the product packaging can be enhanced by a software company.

3. Most software firms have international channels of distribution, enabling the entrepreneur to reach the growing overseas market.

The disadvantages are:

1. The entrepreneur effectively is giving up control over his product since most software firms require eventual product ownership.

2. Usually the entrepreneur also gives up the technology base, which means he or she must start again to build the business.

3. The software company will often require stronger indemnifications and contractual commitments from the entrepreneur than will normal customers.

4. Such arrangements usually have only minimal guarantees.

The general case is that entrepreneurs who develop products and grant rights to software companies are psychologically unhappy but financially rewarded. This is a valid methodology for product launching and should be considered. This topic is covered further in the Appendix.

10.2.5   Publisher/Retail Outlets

Similar to the arrangement just described is the use of retail outlets to distribute mini and microcomputer software. There is a close similarity between this concept and the book publishing industry. The developers, either through a publisher or as a part of their own effort, sign up distributors or retailers. The products are packaged on diskettes with appropriate documentation. The distributor/retailer purchases each system from the developer and marks up the price to obtain a profit.

Even with copyright protection, the developer must be concerned with bootlegged programs. Some security techniques are available. This is a rapidly growing market with a rapidly growing piracy problem.

The software entrepreneur should consider a publisher as another professional who can offer a valuable service and will get paid for that service. Of course, this requires additional royalties and fees, but it does reduce the problem of reaching numerous distributors and dealers. There are several companies that serve as publishers for developers, including a few established software publishers and many new emerging ones. The entrepreneur should certainly consider this as a possible sales source if it fits the product area.

If this chapter does nothing else it should indicate that the "how" question is not easily answered. A workable approach is:

STEP 1. Entrepreneur begins to market the product.

STEP 2. After three or four sales, the entrepreneur brings in a salesperson or agent.

STEP 3. After twelve sales, the entrepreneur chooses to set up a sales force, obtain an agent, work with an existing software company, find a publisher, or work with distributors/dealers.

10.3   WHEN

A primary part of any sales plan is the scheduling of sales events. The events usually include:

1. Product introduction. When should the product be announced?
2. Sales materials. When must product descriptions, sales presentations, and so on be completed?

3. Promotional events. When will advertisements, mailings, or seminars occur?

4. Sales efforts. When will prospects in the geographic area be contacted?

As with any event, timing of each of these is essential. Later in this book we'll discuss each of these events in detail. For now we will briefly discuss timing.

There is little pre-announcement in the software industry. Normally such activities are withheld until the product is tested and complete. There is a good reason for this: Software product deliveries are notoriously delayed. If the entrepreneur is at the end of the tunnel and can see the daylight of completion, then product announcement is a safe bet, provided that other elements of the sales plan are in place.

The sales materials must be prepared to assist the sales process and thus require a special view. Yet they obviously must reflect the final product and should not require extensive reworking. Thus once testing begins it may be appropriate to begin these materials. (We'll discuss what exact sales materials are required later in this chapter.)

Promotional activities should also coincide with product release. Nothing is more difficult than to inform twenty prospects that the product will not be available for months. Promotional activities include press releases, mailings, advertising, and seminars. We'll discuss these also later in this chapter.

Sales efforts probably begin the first day of the entrepreneurial venture. We've already emphasized customer interfaces for product design and other activities. Closing prior to product readiness should be done only with caution, since most prospects do want a finished product. Obviously timing is essential.

10.4 WHERE

Where the product is sold is not as simple a question as it sounds. There is a clear trade-off between a limited geographical introduction and national coverage. Even large software firms with national sales forces sometimes utilize geographic introduction.

The advantage to a limited introduction is that it will minimize the risks associated with sales follow-up, product installation, and customer support. With an increased probability of a happy customer base in a limited geographical area, the entrepreneur can launch a national campaign with a sounder foundation. The disadvantages are twofold. First, the entrepreneur will miss some initial market enthusiasm and thus some business. Second, most users will request local references, thus negating the value of the initial customer base as a nationwide campaign begins.

A national program on the other hand, will likely have more initial sales and build a more diverse customer base. It will also create a greater impact and a better chance of penetration. However, there will be a lower likelihood of "completeness" in coverage and support.

The decision is really a function of resources. If one can sell and support a product on a national basis, then this is a valid approach. The question requires an honest appraisal of skills and resources.

10.5 WHY

It is important to examine why each step is being taken. For example, an ad being placed only for ego fulfillment is really not of value. The "why" should be directed toward making a profit. An ad that is designed to bring in new leads is of value.

A very good approach would be to list each step of the sales plan and to write out why each step is being taken. This detailed analysis can serve as the basis for revision of the sales plan.

In general, most sales and marketing actions should be very strongly questioned. Usually most companies spend enormous amounts of time evaluating technical or financial decisions and relatively little time analyzing sales and marketing decisions. Yet these latter activities are probably the most noticeable to the general public.

10.6 SALES MATERIALS AND AIDS

An important part of the sales plan is the set of sales materials and aids. Although this section does not deal with all of the numerous materials that are required, these are a starting point for initiating discussions.

10.6.1 Product Descriptions

A major ingredient of any software sales program is a set of descriptive materials about the product. Normally, for large computer software a small marketing-oriented product specification and a larger product description are required. For micro and mini systems, a product specification may be sufficient. The marketing-oriented product specification should outline the features of the product, briefly analyze them, and identify the resultant benefits. Some very preliminary technical attributes should be described. The product description should tell the reader what the product does and how it does it in sufficient detail to entice the prospect. This document often is an outgrowth of preliminary design element.

10.6.2 Press Releases

Product announcements in trade journals are a fundamental way of bringing a product to the marketplace. Normally a well-written one- to two-page document sent to the major computer periodicals will result in an article or announcement. A list of addresses can be obtained from normal market source books. Personal contacts are very helpful in getting a release published and in some cases some paid advertising may increase the probability of publication. A personal phone call to the periodical can often assist your effort.

10.6.3 Mailings

Mailings serve as a very useful way to introduce a product and are important enough for us to discuss once again. Mailing lists can be purchased, from any of several vendors and at various costs. Since mailing lists are normally proprietary and protected by copyrights, one should not use a pirated list. There are some free sources of mail lists including local user groups, press releases in computer publications, and personal contacts. The software entrepreneur should add to the lists as new inquiries are made.

A well-done mailing normally consists of a personalized one-page letter, a brief marketing-oriented description, and one or more action items. If a trial is being offered, the mailing usually contains a trial agreement. If not, the action item is usually a reply form on which the prospect is to provide basic information and answer qualifying questions. A postage permit can be obtained from the local post office.

With the cost of travel increasing, mailings are a very important marketing tool. Normally the returns from a mailing based on a qualified list can run as high as 10 to 25 percent. A mailing that is followed up by a phone call will often generate double the normal set of qualified leads. There are several important gimmicks that can be used with mailings. These include:

1. *A self-qualifying reply card.* This is the use on the reply card of two or three boxes which the inquirer checks off. One box states, "Please send detailed information for immediate evaluation." The second might state, "Please send information for evaluation within 30 to 60 days." The final states, "Please send general information." This allows the prospects to qualify themselves as to readiness. Obviously, all replies should be followed up. The ones with an immediate need should be called immediately.

2. *Personalized letters.* The cost of word-processing systems has decreased to the point where personalized letters are a distinct possibility. Many marketeers believe that a personalized letter greatly enhances the probability of an individual's reading it. The reality is that, in any case, a well-written attention-getting letter will be most successful. If you cannot afford a word-processing system, you can consider printing letters on your letterhead and typing the addresses and greetings.

3. *Trial agreements.* A no-cost trial agreement is often offered. At the minimum this agreement should protect the proprietary rights of the product. Many vendors use a trial agreement that automatically converts into a purchase after a given time period.

4. *Requesting the names of other individuals in a company.* If you are selling a product that is geared toward a specific group, such as data-base administration, the reply may request the name of the manager of that group.

5. *A "president's letter."* Some software companies send out a letter signed by the president and stating a specific date and time that the salesperson will call

the prospect. This greatly increases the probability of getting through to the prospect.

6. *A handwritten note.* Some salespeople include a very brief handwritten note stating that they will call within a week. Normally this is a good personal touch.

Again, it should be emphasized that mailings are an excellent way to get through to prospects and should be used in any sales campaign.

10.6.4 Seminar Kits

Almost every software company at one time or another uses seminars to present their products. The reason for this is quite simple: if you can get in front of ten or more companies to tell your story, you will likely sell at least two or three or them.

Appendix D is devoted to How to give a seminar. In this section we will talk about the preparation of a kit to assist in this process.

Normally a seminar will be given in a hotel meeting room and some form of visual displays will be used. These displays are usually flip charts, foils, or slides. In general, the factors determining what media are to be used are cost and audience size. Flip charts work well for up to ten individuals. Foils, or transparencies, are effective for up to twenty. (Foils of computer reports are often illegible beyond ten feet.) Slides are the most expensive media but work well for audiences of all sizes.

The key to any of these forms is that each individual chart, foil, or slide should be brief and make no more than three or four points. Obviously the entrepreneur should spend time preparing and practicing with these materials. A script is normally prepared but this serves only as a guide.

The seminar should be relatively informal, allowing for questions and, of course, creating enough interest so that the attendees complete information requests. There are some vendors who rely entirely on seminars to create interest; they follow up this interest by normal methods.

10.6.5 Survey Selling

An interesting new sales technique has evolved whereby a software company uses either an outside party or an employee to conduct a "nonsales" survey, calling hundreds of prospects and asking nonthreatening qualifying questions, such as:

1. Do you currently use IBM's CICS system?
2. Do you plan to add any applications?
3. Who in your organization is responsible for CICS maintenance?

The result of this survey is a list of well-qualified individuals who are good prospects for a product.

10.6.6 Contract

Section 11.6 in this book is devoted to software contracts. A well-written contract can greatly decrease the time required to close a sale. The preparation of a good contract is an absolute prerequisite for selling.

10.6.7 Packaging

There are numerous individuals and companies who specialize in preparation of sales-related materials, including all of the aids mentioned in this section.

In spite of the availability of this large group of professionals, the entrepreneur should attempt to use such services only if that professional has some computer-related (and preferably software-related) experience.

10.6.8 Advertisements

There are really three basic types of media placement:

1. Placement advertisements
2. Classified ads
3. Press releases

Placement advertising, i.e., display advertising within the normal pages of a publication, is expensive. Some large software companies look to placement advertising as image creating, as opposed to prospect creating. These firms will tell you that an ad never sold a product. Others believe that ads are responsible for 50 percent or more of their business. Many smaller companies tend to create some type of action response, such as telephone inquiries. There currently are little existing data to validate the usefulness of placement advertising. Obviously, if an ad does not generate some leads or reach prospects, it is useless. Yet an ad to announce a product may greatly increase the receptivity of a prospect to the sales. When placement advertising is used, the actual ad should look professionally prepared. Do not hesitate to use an advertising firm to prepare the ad, particularly if you are inexperienced in such work.

Classified advertising is normally found at the end of computer periodicals. It usually costs less than placement advertising and does not normally require prepared artwork. Some smaller companies utilize this type effectively, although as they grow, they begin to use placement advertising.

We have already discussed press releases. They are an excellent way to achieve product announcments.

The style of any advertising can vary from a posed graphic to a simple elaboration of features. Surveys have found that more readers will focus on some form of attention-getting ad and will shy away from overwhelming verbiage.

Advertising is important and can be used effectively. Unless the entrepreneur is creative and has previous experience in this area, however, he or she should consult with a professional.

REVIEW

1. Restate the difference between sales and marketing.

2. Review the five basic "hows" of selling. List each how and state positives and negatives of each.

3. If you have never been on a sales call, contact a software salesperson and ask if you can go on a call with him or her.

4. If you plan on hiring a salesperson, what skills do you (a) require, or (b) prefer?

5. How would you envision working with a rep firm?

6. Would you consider having a major software firm acquire your product?

7. What sales materials do you plan to use?

REFERENCE

1. Frank, A. L., "From Idea to Profit," *Computerworld,* May 5, 1980; May 12, 1980; May 19, 1980; May 26, 1980; June 2, 1980. This is a five-part series of articles on preparing and packaging a computer software product for sales to a larger, existing software firm.

Chapter 11

PRESALES PLANNING
What To Do Before You Begin
to Sell

11.1 INTRODUCTION

Whether you plan on selling your product yourself, with your own sales force, or
through any of the other methods discussed in the previous chapter, before anyone
begins to sell, you need at the very least the following:

1. A list of prospect–suspects
2. Call record forms
3. A sales pitch
4. References
5. Contracts and price lists
6. Promotional material

Although we've already talked about some of these materials as to content, we'll
now discuss them with the emphasis on use. Remember that what you do before you
begin to sell is really a function of how you choose to sell. In some cases, you will not require all of these materials.

11.2 A LIST OF PROSPECT-SUSPECTS

We have mentioned the decision required as to geographical distribution. Regardless of choice, local or national, a list of prospect–suspects is required for the territory. In the computer software industry it is a rare occurrence for a sales territory to be of such a small size that the salesperson goes knocking on door after door on floor after floor in building after building discussing the latest product. The effective salesperson needs a list of suspected prospects, that is, suspects to call on. There are numerous commercial lists available. Some of the better known are provided by:

1. International Data Corporation, Newton, Massachusetts
2. Computer Intelligence Corporation, La Jolla, California
3. Applied Computer Research, Phoenix, Arizona
4. Numerous computer publications such as *Computer Decisions* or *Datamation*

These lists differ greatly in price and content and are geared to the larger (not micro) computer market. Normally each item on the list contains at least one key individual contact, the principal location, the number and type of CPU(s), and sometimes some additional information such as operating systems, product programs, peripheral, and some back-up contact information.

The commercial lists are periodically revised. However, most salespeople have learned not to accept the information as gospel since sometimes names are misspelled, personnel have changed, the company has converted systems, or there are other changes.

Most of these lists will provide you with sample listings. Check out samples prior to purchase. Also ask for references so that you can discuss how others use the data. You may wish initially to purchase a list for only a limited geographical area. If you do this, you can determine whether the total list purchase is of value.

The form of the commercial list varies; it might be full-page computer printouts, prospect cards, labels, books, or computer tapes. If you plan to perform a great deal of analysis, the computer readable form is invaluable provided you can easily access that data.

There are other often overlooked sources of suspects. One major source is the Sunday classified advertisements. In large cities one can frequently find three or more full pages of classified advertisements for programmers. The ads are usually descriptive enough to determine hardware- and software-related matters. Some employment agencies may cooperate with the entrepreneur and provide client contacts. Another source is local user groups, some of whom publish directories. Finally, a very good source is the suspects themselves. A good salesperson will always ask a suspect or prospect if he or she knows of any other prospective customers.

Once a list is obtained or is created from several services, it must be maintained. It is surprising how negligent most computer software firms are when it comes to list maintenance. The notable exceptions are the firms who have greatly reduced their cost of sales. Those firms record every inquiry and document every salesperson's call records. They can then do selective mailings and also provide salespeople with analysis. The best time to create a list maintenance procedure is before you begin to sell.

11.3 CALL RECORD FORMS

As a general procedure, the sales group prepares a call record form with initial basic information. Various companies have their own favorite designs, often with carbonlike copies going to sales management. Other firms (but really too few) will have computer input forms. This serves as the basic prospect reference document for sales analysis and is an ideal source for future marketing research.

A call form should contain current environmental information with transactional entries of sufficient detail to permit a new salesperson to pick up the forms and proceed to take over the account and to permit sales management to review those accounts. The transactional records should include date of call, person with whom the conversation occurred, the basic discussion, and action items. Figure 11.1 is one example of a call record form and the typical notation.

In some firms the actual form may be at the descretion of the salesperson, and so there is some lack of uniformity. This method is not advisable. Uniformity should be enforced as a policy decision.

11.4 SALES PITCH

A good salesperson will have an introductory telephone or in-person sales pitch. Most salespeople agree that if they can follow an outlined presentation on the phone or in person they feel much more comfortable with the call. The presentation should include:

1. *An introduction.* This should clearly state the salesperson's name and company. Normally the first call will avoid laborious introductions and instead move swiftly into the materials.
2. *The purpose.* After the brief introduction the salesperson will wish to state the purpose of the call. This will include product description, personal introduction, determination of interest, and the like.
3. *A summary of the product offering.* The next step is to describe the product by emphasizing the features and the benefits of the software package. On the phone, the pitch is really interest baiting, while in person it can be more specific. There is no common rule as to whether it should be formal or invite interaction. In any case, it should succinctly offer enough information about the product so that the prospect can recognize why he or she might be interested.

CUSTOMER PROSPECT CALL HISTORY

NAME_____

ADDRESS_____

_____ ZIP_____

TELEPHONE_____ EXT_____

CONTACT
NAMES_____ TITLE_____ EXT_____

_____ _____ _____

_____ _____ _____

_____ _____ _____

_____ _____ _____

_____ _____ _____

INSTALLATION
INFORMATION_____

_____

_____

_____

DATE	SPOKE TO	REMARKS
_____	_____	_____
_____	_____	_____
_____	_____	_____
_____	_____	_____
_____	_____	_____
_____	_____	_____
_____	_____	_____
_____	_____	_____
_____	_____	_____
_____	_____	_____

FIGURE 11.1

4. *A qualifying action question.* The salesperson wants to qualify the prospect with a question that invites further action and verified environmental actions. This can be in the form of, ''Would you like more information describing how SuperSoft will function on your IBM 3033?'' If the answer is ''No,'' the salesperson probably wants to change the prospect's mind at least to the point of having the next action be a new call.

5. *A set action step.* The salesperson will want to obtain agreement on an action step such as a future meeting. This should be confirmed with the prospect.

6. *A request for additional prospects.* A good salesperson *always* asks for prospects. Most contacts will respond positively to requests for other names.

7. *A thank you.* Prospects appreciate courtesy, and courtesy provides an excellent image for the new company.

The following is a sample of such a canned sales pitch:

SALESPERSON: Good morning, Mrs. Prospect. My name is Joe Salesman and I'm an Account Manager for S^2, Inc., a new software company. I'm calling today to introduce myself to you and to see if you might be interested in our product. I will be certain to limit our call to only a few minutes.

PROSPECT: I'm very busy today. Can you call back?

SALESPERSON: Of course. I'd be happy to since I'm certain that you'll want to know more about SuperSoft, which can help you maintain all of your operating system software. In fact, most of our users have been able to defer hiring new systems programmers as well as get the job done in a much more responsive manner. SuperSoft automatically applies lines to existing software and tests it. With SuperSoft your programming staff can concentrate on important tasks. Does this seem like it might fit into your own MVS environment?

PROSPECT: Yes, but I don't have more time today.

SALESPERSON: Fine, I would like to meet with you for one-half hour. Would you prefer next Tuesday morning at 9 or Wednesday afternoon at 3?

PROSPECT: I'd prefer to see some literature first.

SALESPERSON: I'd be happy to drop it off on either Tuesday or Wednesday when we meet.

PROSPECT: Can't you mail it to me?

SALESPERSON: Fine, I'd be happy to and then we can discuss the product on either Tuesday or Wednesday.

PROSPECT: You certainly are persistent. I'll see you on Tuesday at 9.

SALESPERSON: (Realizing that he's about to go over the limit.) Thank you. By the way, do you have any suggestions of other executives in your area whom I could contact?

PROSPECT: Try Sam Suspect at PTR, Inc.

SALESPERSON: You've been very helpful. I'll get you the literature and plan to see you on Tuesday the 31st at 9. Thank you very much.

Not every call goes that way, but a script is very helpful in directing the conversation.

11.5 REFERENCES

If possible, the salesperson should not begin any effort without at least one or two local references. The key to using a reference is to be certain that the party will give a good referral. Most salespeople will not use a reference unless within the preceding few weeks they have talked with the reference or have had a trusted associate check the reference. References are valuable and do serve as an important sales tool. An intelligent salesperson will treat references with an almost holy respect and *always* follow up the use of a reference with a thank you.

One problem facing the entrepreneur is that the start-up product offering may not have the extensive reference base of an established software product. Thus it becomes exceptionally important to cultivate sponsor or test sites for a product. These in turn become the basis for initial sales activities. Naturally, these initial references are worth a great deal and should be well serviced.

11.6 CONTRACTS AND PRICE LISTS

Contracts and price lists are very important. Contracts, if properly used, can aid in closing. They can accommodate a trial and present a firm delivery or installation date.

There are several fundamental sections to a license or contract for software:

1. A description of the product, including programs, documentation, and other materials
2. Form of program distribution (that is, source versus object)
3. Maintenance commitments
4. Enhancements versus new releases
5. License grant, including term and conditions of use
6. Payment, including acceptance/testing period
7. Tax payment
8. Delivery and installation responsibilities
9. Warranties of ownership and proprietary rights
10. Limitations of liability

Under no circumstances should you attempt to prepare a contract or license agreement without legal counsel. In order to work with your attorney, you should make some preliminary decisions as to the above issues and then be prepared to discuss these issues. Review the final draft of a contract. Be certain you have asked yourself many "what if?" questions. If you don't like the final contract or license, change it.

Some firms have a separate license and maintenance agreement. The reason for this is twofold. As we will discuss later, there is an industry standard of free first-year maintenance. Thus some companies wait until after the license agreement is signed to present the maintenance contract. Additionally, the larger the contract, the longer the sales cycle. It is conceivable, though, that a singular license and maintenance agreement is sufficient.

Price lists add a credibility to the sales effort. There are normally two types of coexistent price lists. The first is a typeset, nicely formatted list which states the price for software, license, maintenance fees, and any rentals or lease prices, and indicates given policies. The second is a list used only by the sales force and not for distribution since it includes proprietary policies.

Most software is licensed to users. The reason for this has mainly to do with the legal concept of ownership. With normal sale of a product, the purchaser owns the product and is relatively free to do what he or she chooses with it. For historic reasons, the U.S. legal system has attempted to limit any restrictions of non-real estate (as opposed to real estate) property. Thus, instead of selling the product outright, users obtain a license which may be perpetual in duration. Thus the software company may restrict the use of the package to a given CPU and require the user to agree to maintain the confidentiality of the product. There is usually a given set of license fees on the public price list. On the nonpublic price list the software companies often list multiple sales discounts, special maintenance fees, and so on. These are usually for the guidance of the salesperson and are not often presented to prospects.

11.7   PROMOTIONAL MATERIALS

Finally there is promotional material. If the salesperson is unable to follow up the sales call with such material, it is a disaster. The salesperson loses confidence, the suspect is usually disgruntled, and the sale is delayed. This book deals with promotional materials elsewhere.

11.8   SALES PLANS

Any well-prepared salesperson will normally create a sales plan for a one- to six-month period. The contents of such a plan may vary, but normally a sales plan will include:

1. Given goals for weekly prospecting, demonstrations, presentation, personal calls, and proposals
2. Key mailings
3. Seminars
4. Attempts to recycle through given customers, prospects, and suspects

Most computer software sales managers agree that the expected business is a function of the "numbers"—the pipeline previously described. The numbers are prospect calls, sales calls, demonstrations, presentations, and proposals. In most circumstances a salesperson who creates sufficient activity can depend on above-quota performance.

—————————————— REVIEW ——————————————

1. Talk to salespeople to see what lists they use and how they value them.

2. What data do you specifically wish to have on the call forms?

3. Outline a sales pitch for your product idea or for a product idea outlined elsewhere in this book.

4. List ideas of how to get and keep references.

5. Obtain several contracts and review them. Rate them as to the factors listed in this chapter.

6. Prepare a sales plan for your product. If possible, request that known salespeople show you their plans.

REFERENCES

1. Bernacchi, Richard, and Gerald Larsen, *Data Processing Contracts and the Law.* A standard text for data-processing contract law.

2. Bigelow, Robert P., and Susan H. Nycun, *Your Computer and the Law.* Englewood Cliffs, N.J.: Prentice-Hall, Inc., 1975. A good general introduction to computer law.

3. Brandon, Dick H., and Sidney Sigelstein, *Data Processing Contracts.* New York: Van Nostrand Reinhold Company, 1976. A well-done but user-oriented contract guide for data-processing contracts.

4. Fenton, John, *The A to Z of Sales Management.* New York: Amacom, 1979. This is a well-written guide which provides insight on how to organize prior to sales efforts in order to manage the activity.

Chapter 12

SALES
How to Sell a Software Product

12.1 *CHARACTERISTICS OF SALESPEOPLE*

Software sales require a highly individualized and widely varying set of skills. There is no such thing as a typical software salesperson. Software salespeople vary in backgrounds from ex-systems programmers to ex-toilet paper salespeople. Even with such wide backgrounds the successful salespeople have certain common characteristics:

1. *Good organization.* We've already emphasized the need and techniques for organization. Successful software people can give you (either recalling mentally or retrieving from records) detailed information about their current and planned activities. Good salespeople maintain call records, customer files, prospect lists, weekly plans, and forecasts.

2. *Knowledge of product.* All good salespeople are well-trained in their products. They may not understand the internal coding structure, but they certainly know features and benefits. Product knowledge extends to how the product can solve the user's problems as well as how the product compares with competition.

3. *Presentation skills.* All good salespeople continue to work on presentation skills and improvement of techniques. It is difficult to have the customers respect the product if they do not respect the salesperson. Salespeople try different presentation techniques and rehearse their presentation.

4. *Closing orientation.* New salespeople very quickly learn that you do not get the orders without asking for them. All good salespeople are not afraid of asking for the order.

5. *Self-motivating personalities.* All successful salespeople are able to "get themselves up," not only for important calls but also for less interesting tasks such as prospecting or even doing paperwork.

6. *Listening skills.* A good salesperson not only knows when to be quiet, but knows how to listen to customers, is constantly aware of objections as well as buying signs, and copiously takes important notes.

12.2 A CASE STUDY

Before examining these characteristics in detail, we will look at a hypothetical sales situation by following an "average" salesperson through her efforts with "typical" accounts. Barbara Rogers is an ex-applications programmer selling a set of tax accounting systems (installed on minicomputers or turnkey with a proprietary hardware system) for ITAS, Inc. Ms. Rogers sells primarily to small or medium-size accounting firms in the Dallas–Forth Worth area. (We've obviously decided to introduce new cases. The reason for this is simply that we can better illustrate proper sales methodology by not emphasizing the initial T-charts. However, the reader is invited to prepare sales scenarios for those T-charts.)

Barbara has created a suspect list from the local telephone directories, which show over 300 such firms. ITAS, Inc., has not sold in Dallas–Fort Worth before, so Barbara calls her fellow national salespeople to see if any of them have any ex-customers who have moved to her territory. Barbara is lucky in finding that Jerry Baker, a partner of one New York customer, moved to Dallas six months ago. Barbara, with background information regarding that installation, calls the ex-customer, introduces herself, and sets up an appointment to meet with Mr. Baker.

At the appointment Barbara reintroduces herself and ITAS, talks with Mr. Baker about his previous installation, and then gives Mr. Baker a presentation on the newer aspects of ITAS's system.

Fortunately for Barbara, Mr. Baker liked the old ITAS system and had been planning to install a similar system here. Because of the past association, Mr. Baker signs a contract and Barbara has a sale.

Barbara has a local reference account. She now begins to prospect. Each week she has the president of ITAS send a letter of introduction to twenty local suspects. This letter tells a little about ITAS and sets a specific time that Barbara plans to telephone the prospect. Barbara follows each of these up with telephone calls which introduce her, briefly review her product, ask several qualifying questions, set a next action, and thank the suspect; then, after recording all call-related information, she goes on to the next suspect.

In some cases the firms called may request additional information, which Barbara sends. Others are not really prospects and Barbara sends them a thank you note. A few welcome Barbara's call and set up a meeting.

At the first meeting Barbara has a flip chart presentation which gives the features and benefits of the product. Barbara then offers to let the prospect visit Mr. Baker's firm to see the system in operation or, alternatively, to bring the product in for a 30-day trial if they sign a normal license agreement and pay a $1,000 installation charge.

Barbara then presents a "canned" proposal to users. If necessary, she will review the presentation and proposal to answer questions. Barbara is authorized to offer free training if the client accepts the proposal within 30 days. When Barbara presents the proposal, she and the client sit down and list out what steps the client must take to review the proposal. Barbara monitors this review and continues to be in contact with the client.

Barbara gets the signed contract, completes the order materials, and arranges for education. She sends the customer a thank you note to be courteous and goes to the first day of education to be certain all is well. She then periodically visits her customers to thank them, as well as to review their use of the product.

With this example in mind let us begin the analysis of successful common characteristics.

12.2.1 Organization

Barbara Rogers proved to be a very organized salesperson. She reviewed her territory, set out to obtain a friendly account, and then worked her prospect list very methodically, being certain to follow up activities. Naturally she maintained some form of daily calendar that reminded her of activities that should occur and that helped her plan for future commitments. She also maintained detailed call records allowing her to know the current status of each account and permitting her to be prepared prior to calling on these accounts. An organized approach to selling is probably the number one characteristic relevant to success.

12.2.2 Knowledge of Product

The computer software entrepreneur must be certain to arm the sales staff with product knowledge. Barbara Rogers has been certain to know her product. She prepared for product training by reviewing all documentation. She asked many questions, trying to put herself in the place of a potential user. She looked at formal training as something to benefit herself and attempted to learn as much as possible. Barbara always wrote out questions she had about the product to be certain she could find out the answers. She was also methodical in documenting customer questions she couldn't answer, so that she could learn from them as well as respond to the clients. Barbara also discussed competitive products and their sales and made certain she knew their relative strengths and weaknesses.

Note that Barbara had a technical background. Nevertheless, it is unlikely that she would examine the code. A nontechnical salesperson might take the same approach. That salesperson would look at the product as a user and determine the features of the product, analyze them, and be able to point out their benefits.

12.2.3 Presentation

Good presentation skills are very important. Barbara Rogers did prepare for her phone conversations. She probably practiced from a script prior to any phone calls. Normally she followed a format which included:

1. Brief introduction of the caller and the purpose of the call
2. An attempt to gain phone rapport with the prospect
3. A brief presentation of the product
4. One or two qualifying questions
5. A set next action
6. A friendly thank you

For her presentation she used a desk-top flip chart. She used a limited number of charts and made certain each chart made no more than three or four points. She has learned, at the least, to:

1. Be certain to get the names and titles of everyone before the presentation.
2. Make eye contact with each participant and attempt to gear the presentation to each member of the audience.
3. Use a pointer to emphasize certain items.
4. Not recite from the charts, but discuss them.
5. Invite audience participation.
6. Be certain to offer several opportunities to close the prospect.
7. Summarize the presentation.

If Barbara presented handouts she normally would wait till the end of the presentation to avoid having the participants skipping ahead. She would also plan ahead as to how many handouts to bring, since having too few handouts invites participants to wander.

She also realizes that every call is really a presentation and thus she works on them by (1) determining the objectives of the call, (2) planning how to achieve these objectives, and (3) clearly defining her next step.

12.2.4 Closing

Barbara continued to move the client toward closing. The good salesperson is like a master strategist, knowing that victory comes with a successful close; he or she uses tactics to position the prospect for a close and then closes the prospect.

There are numerous closing techniques. A few of them are illustrated below.

1. *The simple close.* In this case, the salesperson simply asks for the order. Believe it or not, this is a very effective technique, accounting for a large majority of the sales.
2. *The wedding march.* Here the salesperson ends the first call with a dialogue that invites the prospect to participate in the evaluation process, to outline the steps for participation, and to set objective times for each step. Then the salesperson promptly marches in before each step, reminds the prospects of their "commitment," and finally asks for the order.
3. *The Ben Franklin close.* Here the salesperson invites and lists objections from the prospect. The salesperson answers each of these and then says, "Now, Mr. Prospect, that I have answered each objection, can I get you to sign the order?"
4. *The sales contest close.* Some salespeople will ask for the order as a personal favor to help make their quota or to qualify for the sales contest prize. Intelligent prospects usually recognize when this is real, since the technique is often overused. The advantage to this technique is in the truth of the statement. The disadvantage is that some prospects resent this personal approach.
5. *The time-dependent close.* Most experienced salespeople actually welcome a preannounced price increase. It enables them to set a natural time closing situation for their prospects. Believe it or not, large companies do respond to being able to save $1,000 and they can often push the paperwork through in enough time to accomplish this saving.

Experienced salespeople can tell you exactly where they are in the closing cycle and what the next step is. Part of successful closing is not taking a "no" to mean a lost sale. Sometimes a "no" means only a problem which, when solved, will lead to a sell. Experienced salespeople will be concerned when the prospect offers no objections. This is usually indicative of either inaction or a decision against the product.

Naturally there is a point when the salesperson believes he has exhausted his sales skills and that a close is unlikely. The ability to write off a prospect is very important, since wasted energy on losing causes benefits no one. In fact, such effort will normally detract from other efforts. Experience should teach this and, in the absence of experience, the salesperson should periodically review his prospects to determine if further effort is justifiable.

12.2.5 Self-Motivation

Barbara has a self-motivating personality. She wakes up in the morning like most human beings. In some way she gears herself up for the day of activity. There is really no one way of doing this. Some people believe in motivational courses, cassette tapes, and movies. Others believe in physical exercise. Some rely on meditation. Others play hard rock music. Whatever works is fine, but something is required. Sales can be a devastating career. Most computer entrepreneurs know of at least one associate who has dropped out. The best way to avoid this devastation is to try a few motivational techniques.

A word of warning about handling disgruntled salespeople. Review what is happening with them and, if necessary, suggest they talk to professional psychologists or psychiatrists. If the day is a drag and nothing gets them up, then sales probably isn't for them and you should find something else for them to do. You must assure them that there is nothing wrong with admitting that they are not cut out to be a full-time salesperson. The key is to get them to recognize their own abilities and limitations. A lot of very mediocre salespeople are excellent entrepreneurs.

12.2.6 Listening Skills

Barbara knows when to be quiet so that the prospect can talk. She is not afraid of what the prospect has to say since she knows she can turn those statements into a valid plan to close the sale. Most prospects give keys as to how they can be sold. By listening, Barbara picks up those keys.

——————————————————— **REVIEW** ———————————————————

1. Review Case A in Chapter 2 and see how John Jones *should* sell his product, according to the suggestions in this chapter.

2. How do you plan to organize your sales activity?

3. Put yourself in the place of a new salesperson. What product knowledge do you require?

4. Role-play a potential customer. What objections to the product do you have? How should the salesperson close these sales?

5. What techniques do you use to motivate yourself? Try a few new ones such as looking at yourself in a mirror and telling yourself how great you are, or making a pact with yourself to achieve certain results.

REFERENCES

There are literally thousands of sales-oriented books. Most are good, and a few are applicable to software. Two of these are:

1. Bender, James F., *How to Sell Well.* New York: McGraw-Hill Book Company, 1961. This is a very good introductory sales how-to book. It is one of the few books that covers some very important topics such as note-taking, letter-writing, creative sales presentations, and so on.

2. Dreyfack, Raymond, *Salesmanship in the 80's.* Radnor, Pa.: Chilton Book Co., 1980. This handbook is very useful for both inexperienced and experienced salespeople.

Chapter 13

SALES MANAGEMENT
How to Get Others to Sell Your
Software Product

13.1 INTRODUCTION

Regardless of which sales vehicle you choose, sales management is important. Many of the same techniques used to manage a sales force can be applied to self-management. Additionally, experienced software entrepreneurs will advise you that should you choose to sell through reps or established software companies, you should manage these activities.

There are four equally important items associated with good sales management: *participation, reporting, follow-up,* and *feedback*. The remainder of this chapter will be devoted to the application of these items to each of the sales vehicles.

13.2 PARTICIPATION

Unlike the case with many managers, such as those in programming or financial activities, with sales managers there is a need to participate in the actual activity—selling. There are two important exceptions to this need. The first is in the case of a truly uncomfortable sales manager–salesperson relationship. The difficult salesperson who cannot get along with the sales manager does not come off well in front of customers. Unless the salesperson requires direct customer help from the sales manager, this individual is better off without customer-oriented management participation, and since the sales manager desires to increase sales, he or she is better off without participation.

Thus, the software entrepreneur had best by very sensitive to his or her relationship with the salespeople. The second exception is in the case of a nonsales-oriented sales manager. Most sales managers came up from the ranks and are usually promoted because of their success as salespeople. Often these sales managers are very good in front of customers. In other cases, the sales managers may have no experience or the wrong kind of experience and thus may be disastrous in front of customers. Perhaps a kind example is the 200 percent quota achiever in New York who is sent to Phoenix to manage an office. If the sales manager's aggressive behavior (which is acceptable in New York) is a negative influence on the customer, then participation should be limited. If you do not have sales experience, consider how well (or how poorly) you come off in front of prospects. If you do not believe you will damage a sales call, go ahead. Remember, though, entrepreneurs are often looked at with awe . . . until they make mistakes. The loss of that awe can result in lost sales. Be cognizant of your abilities.

With these two warnings, it should be pointed out that in 95 percent of the cases participation is a key. Participation can generate:

1. *A team selling approach.* The sales manager is really an asset who can be used to close a difficult account or help break into a new area. An intelligent sales-person recognizes the manager as an asset and will use the manager accordingly. Most high-achiever salespeople frequently utilize their managers to assist them.

2. *A positive reinforcement.* Salespeople are emotionally needy creatures. They face daily rejections. A sales manager can positively reinforce salespeople by complimenting them. This positive reinforcement not only results in additional sales but also reduces turnover and improves morale. Of course, positive reinforcement is an important management technique even for nonsales management.

3. *Training and peer review.* A good sales manager can increase the sales force's effectiveness by active participation in the training and review of the sales process. He or she can suggest new techniques and perform dry runs with the sales-person. Additionally, the sales manager is able to provide relevant and timely suggestions for improvement.

4. *Employee review.* Salespeople are normally ranked by quota performance. Quota achievement is really a function of many factors, some of which are directly under control of the salesperson and some of which are not. Territories vary greatly. So does support. A sales manager who participates in sales activities is in a much better position to access a salesperson's performance and set their quotas and territories. Additionally, participation can greatly simplify follow-up training. Employee review not only evaluates but also suggests ways for improvement. For example, a salesperson may require additional product training yet without participation the sales manager may not recognize this.

Participation is an obvious necessity for an entrepreneur's own sales force. What about reps and software companies? Unfortunately, most rep firms see very little participation from their developer companies. It is as valuable a process for the rep to go on sales calls with the developers as it is for the developer to go with the rep. The rep can learn much about important product features, as well as get a much better feeling for the developer's love of the product. The developer can learn how better to support the reps. Software companies that acquire the rights to a product often do not encourage participation. This is a clear mistake. The product developer should be insistent on some participation and the software firm should welcome that participation. The more successfully acquired software products have a history of developer–acquirer interaction. Often the developer gives seminars, goes on sales calls, and periodically works with sales management to increase sales.

Just as the sales manager should participate with the salesperson, the entrepreneur (if not serving as the manger) should participate. (A note of caution: the entrepreneur should be careful not to circumvent the lines of authority to the manager.) Working with the salesperson, the entrepreneur can convey some very good additional knowledge to this representative.

Participation is not a one-sided affair. Both the salesperson and the entrepreneur/developer/sales manager should gain from this. In summary, the salesperson can learn new approaches and gain from the manager's insight. The manager learns about the salesperson and gets a better feeling of the actual marketplace. With participation, the sales manager and salesperson can relate to current mutual activities and transform that relating to more complex nonmutual problems, thus solving the problem of getting the sale.

13.3 REPORTING

Nothing is hated more by salespeople, and nothing is needed more by sales managers, than reporting. The reasons for this disdain vary from "What is the mattter, don't you trust me?" to "When am I supposed to complete those reports if I'm supposed to be in the field?" Normally the salesperson is victorious in his opposition. Probably the only proven successful management technique for enforcing reporting is to tie in commission and expense compensations to standard reporting. Surprisingly enough, the salesperson does find the time to prepare these reports.

Reporting should include a weekly plan showing what occurred against the previous week's plan, a monthly aged list of outstanding proposals, and a periodic forecast.

The weekly plan should by day and time list the activities planned, stating company name, contact name, and type of call (introduction, sales presentation, technical presentation, demonstration, proposal, contract review, or whatever). The salesperson should report actual events on a weekly basis. Many sales managers require the next week's plan by the end of the previous week.

The uses of these reports are many and include:

1. Activity orientation. Salespeople are forced to plan activities if their sales managers require the sales reports prior to the beginning of the sales week.
2. Achievement orientation. By reviewing actual weekly activities versus planned activities, both the sales manager and the salespeople can evaluate their achievements.
3. Historic orientation. The actual weekly activity report can be compared with call records so the manager can be certain the call records are up to date.
4. Comparative orientation. The manager can compare the reports of all salespeople to be certain their respective levels of activity are similar and to note slumps or changes of work habits.

An aged list of proposals serves several key uses to both the salesperson and the manager. First, in the normal process, sales are not obtained without proposals. Thus, a certain level of proposal activity is a prerequisite to quota achievement. Second, older outstanding proposals can be reviewed to determine closing approaches as well as to increase the salesperson's awareness of possible business. Third, such a list should provide a mechanism for dropping prospects who are unlikely to close. Finally, the salesperson and the sales manager can use this aged list of proposals to generate the required sales projections.

Sales projections are essential to any well-run business. Not only does the sales projection provide basic business information, but it also motivates the salesperson to achieve promised sales. The accuracy of projections vary from salesperson to salesperson. A good sales manager knows how to calibrate the sales projections so that the eternal optimists' and pessimists' reports can be translated into meaningful information.

Normally a sales projection includes, by month for a 90-day period, a listing of expected closings by customer, showing products, dollar values, and probability of close. Many sales managers also require a notice of when this prospect first appeared on the projection as well as a note that a prospect has dropped off.

Obviously, other reporting may be required, including:

1. *Order transmittals.* Normally a contract must be accompanied by some form of transmittal including shipping and environmental data.
2. *Expense reporting.* In most cases, salespeople are reimbursed for expenses and companies require documentation of travel and entertainment expenses.
3. *Proposal copies.* Many companies wish to maintain copies of all proposals submitted.
4. *Major account activity.* Certain companies have multiple computer installations and are referred to as major accounts. Sometimes special master contracts exist. Most software companies emphasize sales to such organizations.

5. *Lost business reports.* It's a proven fact that some sales will be lost. The reasons for this lost business can be very important for product planning and management activities. These reports normally state why business is lost.

Some groups have implemented computerized sales reporting systems which serve primarily to gather the above-mentioned data as well as provide the reports necessary. Normally, however, this is a manual process. As we shall see, good sales managers use these reports to follow up on sales activites. If the reports are not used, there is something wrong with the manager or report.

13.4   FOLLOW-UP

The importance of follow-up, or action items, is obvious. A good sales manager will arrange a list of follow-up items, by salesperson, and will discuss these items with the salespeople on a periodic basis.

The follow-up usually includes:

1. *Review of the week's sales plan.* For example, if the salesperson consistently does not visit with scheduled clients, the sales manager wants to know why.
2. *Proposal follow-up.* Most proposals have some associated time constraints and the sales manager should be certain the salesperson attempts to close within that time.
3. *Support needs.* Typically a salesperson requires home office or field support. The sales manager should continue to see that the salesperson receives assistance as needed.
4. *Review of projections.* Sales managers can normally enhance their projection calibration through careful follow-up.
5. *Psychological presence.* Salespeople are notoriously self-driven and sporadically energetic and thus often need some form of direction. By careful follow-up the sales manager can create this direction.

Follow-up requires systematic record keeping. A good sales manager organizes the follow-up and initiates discussion based on preparation. An executive style daily planner is a must. It can be used not only to record daily activities but also to direct follow-up. Additionally, some sales managers use action numbering schemes. Whatever system is used, the key is organization.

Before leaving follow-up we should examine the effect of bad follow-up. In general, a sales manager's job is to get sales. There are budgetary considerations, personnel development requirements, and coordination decisions. Yet sales achievement is the most important aspect. Poor follow-up not only loses sales but also delays the sales cycle. The sales manager must control the sales force. It's impossible to maintain that control without follow-up. Finally, shoddy follow-up will encourage salespeople not to be concerned about commitments, to get lazy, and eventually not to sell.

13.5 FEEDBACK

Feedback is related to follow-up. The difference is really one of formality rather than substance.

Most sales managers will respond to almost all input from the sales force. This management style takes input such as reports, phone conversations, and requests for assistance and creates a responsive, outgoing mechanism.

For example, when a salesperson submits a proposal, a good sales manager has several key items that may be initiated. The sales manager may automatically:

1. Be certain the salesperson knows the customer's contract approval cycle.
2. Review the proposal for time constraints which may create support scheduling problems.
3. Check call records to review the timing on the account and determine certain key client names.
4. Discuss the closing strategy with the salesperson.
5. Send a personal letter to the account thanking them for the opportunity to submit a proposal.

In many of the normal feedback mechanisms, a good secretary can ease the burden and take over most of the administrative and feedback activities.

13.6 ADMINISTRATION

Some companies use sales administrators to assist both the manager and the salesperson. More creative software companies recognize that the value of a good salesperson can be enhanced through good administrative support subsystems. It is not uncommon for those organizations to have a one-to-one ratio of sales administrators to salespeople. Thus each call can be followed up with a letter, contract, brochure, and other requested materials. Additionally the administrator can assist the salesperson in the reporting requirements. Those administrators often become sales trainees and, with some formal sales education, can grow into productive salespeople.

The extent to which each of these items (participation, reporting, follow-up, and feedback) is applied to the sales vehicle differs with the personal management style as well as the vehicle. Nevertheless, a consistent use of the items is an essential ingredient to good sales management.

Poor sales management will eventually destroy any software firm. As indicated, the entrepreneur should participate in these activities and enforce control mechanisms. He or she should recognize that, just as good programmers do not necessarily make good programming managers, good salespeople do not necessarily make good sales managers. When in doubt, hire an experienced (and successful) sales manager. The results will be well worth the investment.

––––––––––––––––––––––––––– **REVIEW** –––––––––––––––––––––––––––

1. Assume that John Jones (Case A) has progressed to the point where he chooses to build a sales force. Review each of the four elements discussed in the chapter as they apply to his situation. Then answer the following questions:
   (a) Do you believe John should participate in the sales cycle? What can he add? What can he subtract?
   (b) What sales reporting forms does he need to help run business? How will he use each of these?
   (c) What type of follow-up do you expect he will require for his sales process?
   (d) What types of feedback do his salespeople require?

2. Put yourself in the place of a sales manager. How do the four elements fit into your needs?

3. Go to a local computer store as a potential customer. See how the salespeople react with you. If you can, meet the manager and talk to him or her about managing salespeople.

REFERENCE

1. Fenton, John, *The A to Z of Sales Management*. New York: Amacom, 1979. Not only does this book provide material for presales efforts, but it is also an excellent guide for sales management.

Chapter 14

SUPPORT
How to Keep Salespeople
and Customers Happy

14.1 INTRODUCTION

There are three phases of product support: technical sales assistance, product installation, and product maintenance. Successful software entrepreneurs recognize that support is a very important part of the business. Poor support is often the reason software entrepreneurs are unsuccessful. This chapter will deal with all three phases of support.

14.2 TECHNICAL SALES ASSISTANCE

Regardless of sales mode, technical assistance is required. Except for rare cases, most salespeople are not technical experts. Even when very talented technically, the wise salesperson normally wishes to avoid the technical guru rule. Thus, normally a salesperson welcomes the technical assistance required during the sales cycles. Many sales agents have not created their own technical support groups and the software company using sales representatives usually provides some form of technical assistance. In the case of a software company's marketing of the entrepreneur's product, the company will eventually assume all phases of technical support. However, even those organizations welcome initial assistance in precontract activities.

There are three basic forms of presales assistance: question answering, technical presentations, and product demonstrations.

Question answering is a typical part of the sales cycle. Normally a salesperson will first make a sales presentation, which is usually oriented toward the benefits of the features. If the sales presentation is a good one, the prospect will be interested and will have questions beyond the salesperson's knowledge of the product. These questions, as well as the questions that come up during the prospect's evaluation, are answered by some form of technical support personnel. In some cases, the technical support group will directly interface with the customer. In other instances, the salesperson will respond to questions.

A good way to ease this question-answering burden is to prepare a list of frequently asked questions with the answers. As additional questions are asked, the entrepreneur will add to the master list and distribute the new questions and answers to the sales force.

Even with this background, special technical presentations are useful. Many salespeople choose to use technical presentations as part of their sales cycle. This provides an opportunity to convince the prospect of the product's technical superiority. The presenter is often subject to vigorous questioning. A technical presentation is really an offensive (that is, aggressive) tactic. The presenter must be polished and competent. If the salesperson is experienced, he or she will brief the presenter regarding the account and what they hope to accomplish.

Frequent success stories in the software industry are due to very good technical presentations. The better software companies prepare these quality presentations. Initially the entrepreneur/developer will provide technical presentations. Ultimately, the company will hire and train a technical support staff, which must consist of verbal, technically competent individuals. The recruiting of such a group is not as easy as it may sound since the average personality profile of programmers does not usually include a desire to communicate with others. As a result, some software firms have hired less technically experienced programmers (with one or two years experience) who wish to be salespeople or consultants. Even after such a group is recruited, their success will require good management. The conflicts arising between salespeople (who are usually paid commissions) and technical sales support (who are often on a salary) are not trivial. Scheduling of support is essential. Finally, and most important, a career path must be offered to this group since there is an unusually high burnout rate.

Often software organizations wish to use product demonstration to help sell the product. There are a few basic reasons for this. First, if the product provides reports, there is a good chance to generate user enthusiasm. Many a product has been sold because a computer executive has fallen in love with a report that he really "must" have. Second, the product can usually demonstrate some immediate benefit. If it can show a cost saving or solve a problem, the evaluator can be a hero and the project is easily justifiable. Third, a good demonstration can shorten the sales cycle by proving the product works in the user environment. Fourth, a good demonstration can get the prospect accustomed to using the system. Fifth, a demonstration can generate useful closing materials. A proposal can be geared to the results of that demonstration.

Some software companies have their salespeople perform their demonstrations, but most utilize technical support people to perform these tasks. As previously mentioned, the technical support individual is very important. He or she must be technically competent. It's hard to recover from bringing down the user's system when you're trying to impress the user's management. The technical support person works with user personnel. This is an excellent opportunity to create a friendship. In some ways the use of technical support can complement the user technical staff by creating an atmosphere of camaraderie between the technical support individual and the user. Finally, the technical support person should be motivated to help get the sale. Where demonstrations are used, the technical support group can make or break a sale. Many a salesperson has provided the technical support engineers with excellent wines.

The presales use of technical support is not a luxury. It is a necessity. Such individuals should be competent, people-oriented and motivationally compensated. Although a technical sales support staff is a characteristic of a mature software firm, it is also a requirement for a growing firm.

14.3 PRODUCT INSTALLATION

Once a contract is obtained, the product still must be delivered and installed. There may be truly off-the-shelf software, but it is rarer than might be believed. Someone must be responsible for seeing that the product shipped is the correct version for the user and that, if necessary, certain customizations occur.

Software companies are split evenly in their installation policies. Many products are user-installed. In those cases, there are normally installation procedures and someone who is available to answer users' questions and solve their problems. In other instances, the software company has its own designated technical support person to perform the installation. In most cases, training is available.

The installation/training process may be a free item or it may be billed to the customer. In any case, whether user-installation and self-education occur or custom installation and training occur, it is very important to see that the customer experiences a successful taste. For one thing, most contracts warrant that a product will work and the client can cancel if installation is not successful. Second, there is a normal company resistance to new systems, and initial problems are usually not forgotten. Also, every customer should be a valuable reference. A software entrepreneur does not want an unhappy user to stand up at a local computer meeting and recount what a terrible time his company had getting the entrepreneur's product to work. Finally, every customer is a prospect for further products and enhancements. Thus, the software company has a strong motivation to work with the user during testing and installation.

14.4 PRODUCT MAINTENANCE

With most normal large-scale software sales, the product is maintained at no additional charge for the first year of use. After that, there is a yearly charge which is usually a function of sales price, currently varying from 10 to 20 percent of sales price per year. Exact policies differ, but typically the user or vendor may cancel this maintenance at yearly renewal time. Such maintenance almost always provides for fixing program errors and for pure maintenance releases. Some software companies also include enhancements and some additional features. In other cases, they charge for additional features.

There are several reasons for providing good maintenance:

1. There is a contractual commitment to provide a certain level of maintenance and support.
2. Prospects use existing users as a basis for evaluation of procurement. Maintenance and the ability of the vendor to supply support are usually among the aspects evaluated.
3. Current customers may be future prospects for additional products. Thus, their happiness is very important.
4. Maintenance is a very important basis of a software company's revenue. Thus, long-term profit can be greatly affected. For example, assume Company A is selling 25 $10,000 products per year, so new product sales remain level at $250,000 per year, and a 10 percent per year maintenance charge exists. By the fourth year there would be $100,000 in maintenance revenue. This is a very significant, *repetitive* source of income.

There are varying philosophies as to how to provide maintenance. One model is to have a nonisolated development and maintenance group. A customer calling in would talk to someone from this group. The advantages to this are:

1. The customer deals directly with an author who likely is able to solve the problem.
2. The development/maintenance group is directly attuned to problems and can revise new releases.
3. The development/maintenance group may be aware of similar problems and can be more helpful.

The disadvantages are:

1. The group may be distracted from its efforts of development.
2. Most development groups are not known for their patience or tact. Thus, customers may occasionally be put off.

In another model there is a phone-based customer support representative, a separate maintenance group, and a development group. All customer contact is handled by the customer support representatives, who directly interfere with the customer and a maintenance support group. Only in very difficult circumstances do maintenance engineers deal with the customer. In extremely rare situations, the development group may get involved in the problem-solving area.

The advantages to this are:

1. The customer support reps are normally trained in dealing with the public and thus can treat the client with tact and friendliness.
2. The customer support group is dedicated to this effort. Thus, they spend more time and effort on the task and are not being distracted from other functions.

The disadvantages are:

1. It is very difficult to train these individuals and thus the customer service representatives are not able to respond quickly to inquiries.
2. The remoteness of the development group often leads to less concern for the product quality.

Both methodologies work and yet each requires different management styles. In the usual case a company begins with the nonisolated development/maintenance groups and progresses to the more structured mode. This is usually because the management of numerous larger projects coupled with a growing customer base dictates an isolated development, maintenance, and support agreement.

Whatever style is chosen, the entrepreneur must realize that maintenance is a very important part of the overall software business. A plan should be developed and customers should know to whom they can inquire.

14.5 CRISES

There are numerous reasons for crises in the life of software ventures. Without a doubt, many major crises can be overcome by beginning with and enhancing support mechanisms. If you doubt this, reflect for a moment on the plight of the system software firms when IBM announced their MVS operating systems. More than a few hours in overtime were put in by software entrepreneurs to survive that change. Without good support functions, such a transaction could have literally wiped out many existing firms.

──────────────── **REVIEW** ────────────────

1. How do you plan to support your salespeople from a technical standpoint?

2. Have you considered demonstrating your system? If so, what can you do ahead of time to ensure a successful demonstration?

3. How will your product be installed? Who will install it?

4. Review your budget to reflect the cost of support and maintenance. Does maintenance pay for itself?

5. Which model of maintenance do you propose to utilize?

REFERENCE

1. Gannon, Thomas A., *Product Service Management*. New York: American Management Association, 1972. This is a manufacturing-oriented book. However, it provides good advice on organization, measurement and evaluation, and budgeting and planning.

Chapter 15

FOLLOW–ON BUSINESS
What To Do After the Applause
Dies Down

15.1 INTRODUCTION

It does not require a computer simulation model to prove that with a limited marketplace (such as 3,000 plus large-scale IBM systems or 50,000 plus business microcomputers), in order to build a business, one must have follow-on sales. Most successful software entrepreneurs recognize this and repeatedly bring out additional offerings to the current customer base. No guide to software entrepreneurship would be complete without an examination of follow-on business.

There are two basic ways to generate follow-on business: enhancements and new products.

15.2 ENHANCEMENTS

The definition of an enhancement is one of the most controversial used by software planners. We've already alluded to the fact that enhancements are somehow related to maintenance. The difficulty with any definition of enhancements is that relationship. Outside the software industry an enhancement is a new feature to an existing product. In fact, one school of thought in the software business adheres to this definition. The other school of thought states that an enhancement is really something that adds substantial value to the product.

This argument is based on a financial issue. Often software maintenance fees will exclude enhancements so that the enhancements may be separately charged for. A customer purchases a software product, maintenance keeps that product working, and new features are charged for almost as if they were separate products.

Some software companies have successfully introduced a major enhancement contract whereby the user not only agrees to purchase a license and sign a maintenance agreement, but also agrees to a major enhancement contract. Where enhancement contracts are not used, most software companies normally will market the enhancements as separately priced options. However, there are some firms that include all enhancements as part of the normal maintenance.

The treatment of enhancements is a business decision that should be dealt with in the early life of the software company. Several existing firms have some very early contracts in which they agree to provide all future options at no additional cost, although they now no longer subscribe to that policy. This is not only an adverse financial problem, but also a sales and administration nightmare.

Given that enhancements are a necessary component of any business, how does one determine what is necessary?

We have suggested the concept of an enhancement list during the development period in order to stabilize the development. This list provides an excellent starting place for enhancements. Another obvious source is existing users, who will gladly suggest new features to be provided. Some of these suggestions will be volunteered. However, most software firms formalize this process, either through periodic customer contacts, customer boards of technical advisors, or customer groups.

The periodic customer contacts may be initiated by the company's marketing function in order to determine user satisfaction as well as user requests. In other cases, the customer support function might ask the users what enhancements they would like. Also, more experienced salespeople continue to ask customers for product enhancement ideas and report these to the development groups.

A few software companies have established boards of technical advisors made up of their customers. Such boards not only review technical decisions but also serve to suggest enhancement ideas. The difficulty with this approach is that some companies have policies prohibiting such participation.

Customer user groups are an excellent source for enhancement ideas. This is normally a very formalized procedure. The first couple of meetings are company-run affairs lasting several days and featuring company speakers, user panels, open dialogues, and, of course, social events designed to encourage informal discussions as well as to be entertaining. Such meetings usually take place once or twice yearly with normal participation by several user personnel per site. After the first several meetings, the users begin to take over the management of the meetings with some vendor funding. One regular event of each user meeting is a formal request for enhancements with some type of software company response.

Once the ideas are obtained, the company must begin to evaluate and rank them. With customer input, a major part of the market research is complete. Another source becomes the lost business reports, which often list needed features that are absent. In some cases, firms choose to use additional market research to determine enhancement plans. Normally in a well-run organization there is sufficient input to preclude the necessity for very detailed market research. The ranking of enhancements is determined not only from market-oriented input, but from resources available to the company. Usually a company can budget only a limited number of people days to enhancement. Thus only a certain number of enhancements are possible.

The enhancement project is usually run in a manner similar to the development project, with comparable project controls and management methodology. A word of warning, however. Sometimes the treatment is more destructive than the illness. A five-day enhancement programming effort may not justify an associated fifteen-day planning and control mechanism.

15.3 NEW PRODUCTS

Probably one of the major milestones in the life of the software entrepreneur is the decision to bring out the *second* product. Most experienced entrepreneurs insist that even with a large capital base and a proven organization, a new venture should bring out only a single initial product. This does not preclude careful planning to facilitate secondary offerings.

There are very few single-product firms in the software industry. There are a few simple reasons for this:

1. Once a certain level of penetration is reached by a single product, there is a limited growth potential.
2. Normally once a sales organization is built up, it can absorb additional products and increase sales with little additional cost.
3. Competition will often catch up with a technically advanced product, usually jumping ahead of an existing product offering.
4. Technical gurus enjoy new product development and may drive the company into continued product advancements.
5. Existing customers are an excellent source of new product ideas and are usually receptive to additional product sales.
6. Technological changes invite new product inventions and thus product offerings may be correlated to new hardware releases.

New product decisions are a nontrivial portion of any business growth. The typical firm has clear-cut first product ideas. Expanding an existing product line involves a complex analysis, and adding a new product line is even more complex. The total analysis of both of these questions is well beyond the scope of this book.

However, a brief discussion of this analysis is a necessary component of any software entrepreneur's background.

First of all, there is a well-defined difference between product lines. Normally each set of product lines will be designed to address certain subsegments of the software marketplace. For example, the large-scale computer software marketplace is divided into major segments. One breakdown might be:

1. *Systems tools.* Software that interfaces with the CPU's system control programs or is used primarily to assist in the operation of the computer.

2. *Programming aids.* Software that a programmer would use to develop applications systems.

3. *Applications packages.* Software that performs certain application functions.

Let's say a firm chooses to offer packages that are programming aids. One product line may consist of data-base/data-communications monitors. A second product line may consist of program development tools including screen generators, program generators, and documentation aids. Another product line may be geared toward program testing and maintenance.

The company that brings out a data-base package may choose to expand its product line by adding a data dictionary system. This decision is somewhat similar to that of adding an enhancement in that users, lost business, and initial market survey indicate a need for it. The economic analysis becomes a review of the proposed new product activity.

There are a few key points to product analysis. The most accepted mode of analysis is, as best as possible, to model the business without the product and then with the additional product. Interrelated variables can be accounted for. For example, an addition of a data dictionary system may decrease the total sales of a data-base system because of limited capacity of the sales force. It may shorten the sales cycle and thus bring about higher total sales. Also it is quite possible that a new product introduction may outmode the current support organizations. One way of modeling this effect is to have input from each functional group as to the pros and cons of a new product.

Although a detailed simulation model would be most useful, most software companies do not have detailed simulation models that allow for "what if" questions. However, analysis of the product addition is usually performed with adjustments to the basic company plan to reflect these interactions.

Some companies only perform incremental analysis showing additional sales, detailing costs, and evaluating product profitability. There is a difficulty inherent in this procedure because of the above-mentioned interactions. Yet even incremental analysis is very useful.

A new product decision becomes somewhat more complex when it involves the acquisition or development of a product. It is now commonly acceptable for software firms to look to outside development firms to provide products. In those cases the acquiring firm will review:

1. *Contract terms.* There may be very specific buyer-software company requirements such as ownership or assumption of all existing contracts. Many authors do not wish to relinquish total control.

2. *Financial terms.* The economies of most ongoing software firms is such that only 15 to 30 percent of direct sales can be allocated to royalties on product acquisitions.

3. *Product quality.* The support of a new product requires resources and creates exposure for the acquiring company, thus necessitating a comprehensive evaluation.

4. *Market readiness.* Normally a product developed outside requires repackaging, sometimes to an extent that can influence the date of release.

Thus the addition of a product to a product line requires detailed analysis of the proposed product whether developed internally or externally.

New product lines require not only quantitative analysis but also strong qualitative concerns. The new product line is part of a strategic planning process which cannot be condensed into one simple set of rules. For purposes of analyzing new product lines, one should consider at least:

1. *Effect on existing sales force.* Can the same sales force be used to market the new set of products or must a new group be built?

2. *Customer fit.* Can existing customer installations be approached for these products?

3. *Safety.* Will the new product line be affected by the same set of extraneous factors?

4. *Growth.* Is the new product area one of future growth?

5. *Ability.* Is the necessary technical support available?

6. *Competition.* Will the new product area be in a highly competitive marketplace?

7. *Psychology.* Will a new product line negatively impact morale and team spirit?

8. *Cash flow.* Can the company support the cash necessary to bring forth a new product line?

9. *Personnel needs.* Will the existing personnel be able to support the new product line with controlled addition?

10. *Organization structure.* Can the existing company superstructure support the product line?

The addition of products, product lines, and enhancements is a very important part of the growth of a software firm. These additions are the second hurdle in the growth of a firm and the prepared software entrepreneur will be anticipating this hurdle.

1. How do *you* define an enhancement? Will you charge separately for that enhancement?

2. What are the valid sources for enhancement ideas?

3. Are you willing to bring out an initial single product? If so, how do you plan to follow that effort? If not, how can you justify your decision?

4. Are your new product ideas part of the same product line?

5. Look at John Jones's product. What enhancements can you envision? What new product offerings to the same product line? Is a product designed to help systems programmers write code part of the same product line?

REFERENCE

1. Wachs, William, *99 Ways to Get More Sales from Existing Customers*. West Nyack, N.Y.: Parker Publishing, 1978. This is a very good book outlining *how* to get the follow-on business.

Chapter 16

THE REWARDS

16.1 INTRODUCTION

Software entrepreneurs become software entrepreneurs in order to gain the rewards associated with their business enterprises. In some ways, the software entrepreneur should concentrate on obtaining the rewards. There are a few very good reasons for this emphasis. First of all, when goals are set, the probability of success is enhanced. Second, the reward orientation helps to enforce our fundamental rule of software entrepreneurship. Finally, by keeping in mind the goals, an entrepreneur possesses a much more positive mental attitude. There are three fundamental rewards: income, equity, and satisfaction. The first two of these can be quantitatively measured; the last is strictly a qualitative factor.

16.2 INCOME

Almost everyone is familiar with certain forms of income. As an employee, the professional has received a salary from his or her employer. Even this fundamental form of income brings to bear two major distinctions which deserve discussion. These are gross and net income. To illustrate these we will use the concept of employee earnings. The employee's salary is a *gross income,* the income received prior to any required or optional deductions. The amount of the paycheck is *net income,* the payment received by the employee after all deductions. The deductions are of three types: required governmental taxation, including federal, state, and local taxes; fringelike deductions, including insurance and retirement plans; and optional savings, which may be credit union deductions or automatic transfers.

The employee has control over many of these deductions. With careful tax planning, the employee can reduce some of the tax deductions. For example, an employee can estimate deductions and, by consulting an IRS table, increase normal deductions and thereby increase net spendable income. Some fringe benefit deductions are also controllable. The employee can analyze an optional life insurance plan to determine its desirability and refuse this deduction, increasing the net income. The same is obviously true for voluntary deductions such as savings plans or stock purchase plans.

Another important distinction is that the employee's true gross income (i.e., spendable income plus benefits) exceed the gross pay received. Most employers offer between 10 and 20 percent of net salary as additional fringe benefits, such as company-paid insurance. Thus true gross is a quantitative element that can be measured with analysis.

As the entrepreneurs begin their business, they should be quick to recognize that certain perks are normal and allowable. For example, reimbursement of legitimate (IRS-allowable) business expenses are actually part of their compensation. Proper business planning and analysis permits these business expense reimbursements to be tax-free to the entrepreneur and yet be deductible as an expense by the corporation. What is legitimate is subject to current IRS regulations. For example, under proper circumstances, if the entrepreneur uses an automobile solely for business purposes, the company may lease a car or purchase a car for him or her. Many experienced business-people obtain receipts and documentation for every expense in order to facilitate the justification of business-related perks. There is nothing illegal or immoral about maximizing valid business deductions. Most software entrepreneurs spend more than one sleepless night attempting to find funds to pay for expenses. There is no reason to give away hard-earned income. Rather than dwell on what is a legitimate business expense, we strongly urge the entrepreneur to consult with a tax advisor.

There are other forms of income available to the entrepreneur beside salary and expenses. As a stockholder–owner of the corporation, the entrepreneur may receive dividends. There is a strong divergence of opinion as to payment of dividends.

First of all, there are federal tax rules which, in essence, require payment of dividends in certain situations through the concept of a penalty tax on excessive earnings accumulation. The Internal Revenue Service recognizes that in some situations in order to avoid payment of taxes by its shareholders, a corporation may not wish to pay dividends. In some situations, this is permissible. In others—prohibited purposes—a penalty tax is assessed as outlined in IRC 531. We've already mentioned this, but we will examine it in more detail. There are four aspects of determining a prohibited purpose. These are stated in IRC 532, which begins, "The accumulated earnings tax imposed by section 531 shall apply to every corporation (other than . . .) formed or availed of for the purpose of avoiding the income tax with respect to its shareholders or the shareholders of any other corporation, by permitting earnings and profits to accumulate instead of being divided or distributed. . . ."

Although we won't examine each aspect, we must note that there is a burden on the part of the corporation by a preponderance of the evidence of the purpose. If the corporation accumulates assets that seem to be beyond the reasonable needs of the business, the corporation must prove otherwise. There are certain allowable reasons for accumulation of assets:

1. To provide for expansion or replacement of the business or its plant
2. To acquire a business enterprise through purchasing stock or assets
3. To retire indebtedness
4. To provide working capital
5. To invest or lend funds to suppliers or to customers in order to maintain the business of the corporation

There are numerous theories as to what amount of assets is necessary. If substantial retained earnings exist and the entrepreneur does not plan to issue dividends, the management should be certain to consult their tax practitioner.

The obvious tax planning decision is normally to have sufficient earnings to pay maximum expenses first, then maximum compensation, leaving enough in retained earnings to operate the business in future years. The reason for this is that, as mentioned in an earlier chapter, dividends are doubly taxed. We will now illustrate some of these concepts through examples.

Let's assume that the corporation and individual are taxed and that for calculations, calendar year 1980 tax rates apply.

Assume the corporation's sales are $500,000, with nonentrepreneur-related expenses of $200,000.

In Case A, the entrepreneur is paid $150,000, incurs another $50,000 in legitimate expenses, with $100,000 being retained as working capital.

In Case B, the entrepreneur is paid $100,000, incurs another $50,000 in legitimate expenses, and receives a $50,000 dividend. The company retains $100,000 for working capital.

In Case C, the entrepreneur is paid $100,000, he or she incurs $100,000 in legitimate expenses, and the company retains $100,000 in working capital.

A very simplified tax analysis of these three situations is given in Figure 16.1.

Obviously the entrepreneur wishes to maximize the nontaxable compensation and minimize dividends. There may be some situations when despite the tax implications, the company wishes to pay dividends. These include:

1. To avoid the retained earnings tax
2. To compensate investors (although most sophisticated investors do not look to an entrepreneurial company to pay dividends)
3. To establish an image of a mature company

CASE A

Corporation Taxable Income Analysis

Sales:	$500,000
Less: expenses & salaries	400,000
Taxable income:	$100,000

Corporate Tax Analysis

17% of 1st $25,000	=	$ 4,250
20% of 2nd $25,000	=	5,000
30% of 3rd $25,000	=	7,500
40% of 4th $25,000	=	10,000
Tax due	=	$26,750

Corporation Retains

$100,000 − $26,750 = $73,250

Entrepreneur Analysis

Salary $150,000
taxed at 50% (maximum earned income) = $75,000

Entrepreneur Retains

$75,000 + $50,000 (expenses) = $125,000

Dual Usable Income

$73,250 + $125,000 = $198,250

CASE B

Corporation Taxable Income Analysis

Sales:	$500,000
Less: expenses & salaries	350,000
Taxable income:	$150,000

Corporate Tax Analysis

17% of 1st $25,000	=	$ 4,250
20% of 2nd $25,000	=	5,000
30% of 3rd $25,000	=	7,500
40% of 4th $25,000	=	10,000
46% of remaining $50,000	=	23,000
Tax due	=	$49,750

(continued)

FIGURE 16.1 Case analysis of salary and dividends

CASE B (*continued*)

Corporation Retains

$150,000 − $49,750 (tax) − $50,000 (dividend) = $50,250

Entrepreneur Analysis

Salary $100,000
taxed at 50% (maximum earned income) = $50,000
Dividend $50,000
taxed at (estimated) 70% = $35,000

Entrepreneur Retains

$50,000 + $15,000 + $50,000 (expenses) = $115,000

Dual Usable Income

$50,250 + $115,000 = $165,250

CASE C

Corporation Taxable Income Analysis

Sales:	$500,000
Less: expenses & salaries	400,000
Taxable income:	$100,000

Corporate Tax Analysis

17% of 1st $25,000 =	$ 4,250
20% of 2nd $25,000 =	5,000
30% of 3rd $25,000 =	7,500
40% of 4th $25,000 =	10,000
Tax due =	$26,750

Corporation Retains

$100,000 − $26,750 = $73,250

Entrepreneur Analysis

Salary $100,000
taxed at 50% (maximum earned income) = $50,000

Entrepreneur Retains

$50,000 + $100,000 (expenses) = $150,000

Dual Usable Income

$73,250 + $150,000 = $223,250

FIGURE 16.1 (*continued*)

A yet unmentioned but valid reason for taking income out of a going business entity is that the intelligent entrepreneur will likely wish to put these funds to use. There is a usual pattern associated with a growing, successful computer software firm. The first few years are normally ones of taking only necessary income from the company. When the company begins to get successful, the income is usually increased as good planning dictates. At that time most entrepreneurs, because of their inherent nature, begin to invest in other activities. Normally, because of the time constraints of management, the entrepreneur becomes an investor. In fact, one of the major sources of individual venture capital is successful entrepreneurs. Therefore a valid reason to take income from the corporation is to invest in other entities with the belief that the company will continue to generate income and increase in value through equity.

16.3 EQUITY

The entrepreneur also holds stock in his or her company, and this stock, or ownership interest, represents equity. The value of this equity is a function of the worth of the corporation.

There are numerous ways to assess the value of a corporation. For example, one could look at the after-tax income of the company and assess a valuation as a function of that income. The problem with this is that the multiples used to value a company vary greatly. Most investors in start-up computer software firms use values of 10 and above. Thus a company with a $50,000 after-tax profit might be valued at $500,000.

Another way of valuing the company is to examine its balance sheet and create a value that reflects the company's net worth. Since most software firms' expenses involve software product-development, their net worth is usually not a realistic estimate of value, due to a zero valuation of software as an asset.

Another approach is to look at similar companies for which a public market exists or which have recently been sold, and determine what the value of this firm is by analogy. This analysis usually yields a value that is a function of sales or income. These functions vary greatly with stock market fluctuations, but for a five-year-old company with at least two years of profit, normal values range from one to two times annual sales or ten to fifteen times annual earnings.

Equity is an interesting concept. A company may wish to acquire another company by trading stock, or it may wish to raise additional capital. The difficulty is that the only objective measure of equity in these cases is what someone will pay for the stock. Thus, if the stock is publicly traded, the value of the equity is realistically ascertainable. In fact, the multiples for valuation of publicly traded firms is usually higher than those for firms that are not publicly traded.

The U.S. Congress has passed several acts of legislation to protect the unsophisticated investor from possible abuse and loss. These laws deal with the regulation of the issuance and trading of securities. Similar laws exist in individual states. Because of the divergent rules associated with areas and the *severe financial* and *criminal* penalties that are associated with failure to comply with these rules, the entrepreneur is advised to seek legal counsel prior to beginning the planning for these efforts. Thus, we will deal only with a few concepts and again emphasize that in no way should the entrepreneur act on his or her own behalf in these matters.

Normally in order to sell stock to the public, the company must register its offerings with the Securities and Exchange Commission and the state agency. The complexity of this registration procedure is normally a function of the size of the offering. Usually, complete disclosure of business status is required, as are audited financial statements. In the usual case a company will work with an underwriter, who will coordinate the offering for a fee, usually equal to a percentage of the offering, and in most cases warrants or options for additional stock at a fixed price.

The ability of a firm to raise money from a public offering is usually dependent on a history of growth, several years of earnings, and annual sales of at least $10 million and most often $20 million.

There are several basic reasons for a company to make a public offering. The first is to raise additional working capital for the company; normally a company will use the capital for growth-oriented activities. The second is to have public stock in order to use additional shares for acquisition of companies; publicly traded stock usually is valued at a higher multiple. The third is to allow the founders and investors to receive value for their stock; most people who invest in a software firm do so in order to get many times over their initial investment.

Earlier in the book we discussed the concept of capital gains. If the entrepreneur holds stock in a company and then sells that stock, the funds derived are taxed at a reduced rate. Thus, the entrepreneur certainly usually wants to sell a portion of his stock.

There are some valid reasons for not making a company public:

1. Most public companies must provide extensive quarterly reporting. Major shareholders and officers are subject to limitations on their activities. Finally, the company must disclose many previously private matters.
2. A public company can be acquired by another organization which purchases sufficient stock. Such acquisition attempts are sometimes unsolicited and often bitterly fought contests.
3. The entrepreneur normally gives up some control and thus may lose interest in the company. He or she may also find that personal compensation and activities are limited.

In past years the principal reason software entrepreneurs began companies was to build equity. There are other reasons. Yet even today many entrepreneurs will tell you that their biggest money was the receipt of a seven-figure check from an underwriter after the first public offering.

16.4 SATISFACTION

Building a company is a lot of hard work. Most entrepreneurs put all or most of their personal funds into their venture. Most work in excess of 70 hours per week and carry briefcases full of work home. Most entrepreneurs use a large share of their personal contacts to launch the business. Finally, and probably most important, most entrepreneurs put an extremely high level of psychological energy into their effort.

Software entrepreneurs are very competitive. Some translate this competitiveness into every activity; others focus all their competitiveness into their business. It's very pleasurable to win. A successful business is really a victory.

The satisfaction associated with a successful business leads to respect in the business community. Most successful entrepreneurial efforts also lead to success of other individuals. A $10 million company usually employs over one hundred people. Additionally, there are a few key employees whose wealth through stock ownership is greatly increased by the company's success. Computer software continues to increase in importance as part of the local and national economies.

There is a famous saying that nothing succeeds like success. This is particularly true in the case of an entrepreneur. Success in the software industry is achievable. If the entrepreneur's initial effort is unsuccessful, he or she can rest assured that the next effort has an increased probability of success. Although first-time ventures can and do succeed, some very successful entrepreneurs have one or two prior failures to their credit.

Personal satisfaction is an essential ingredient to a business venture.

--- REVIEW ---

1. Examine your own personal situation with your current or previous employer. List all elements of income including fringe benefits. Place a total evaluation on these elements.

2. List perks you would like. Then think about the legitimate business purposes associated with each of these.

3. Review your company's financial projections. Are there ways to reduce taxation? If so, readjust your plan.

4. Review the concept of usable income. Be certain you can calculate this for your own venture.

5. Obtain the prospectus for one or two software firms. (This is the document prepared concurrent with a public offering.) Determine, if you can, how the underwriter arrived at the valuation for the company.

6. What are your own goals? Write them out and review them.

REFERENCES

1. Brown, Deaver, *The Entrepreneur's Guide*. New York: Macmillan Publishing Co., Inc., 1980. This provides a good view of the entrepreneurial world at large.

2. Bruce, Richard, *The Entrepreneurs, Strategies, Motivations, Successes and Failures*. London: Libertarian Books, 1970. Although this is the British view, it is quite applicable to the many types of entrepreneurs and their motivations.

Appendix A

VENTURE CAPITAL

The software entrepreneur is often faced with a common problem: the money necessary to fund a start-up venture far exceeds the entrepreneur's resources. We have already discussed self-financing. We have also mentioned that other sources may be used by a software entrepreneur to fund a venture. We will identify those funds collectively as venture capital. It is important to distinguish between *venture capital* and *venture capitalists*. The former includes various sources of funding. The latter is a unique group of individuals who specialize in providing funding to new companies.

For purposes of our analysis we will examine four major sources of venture capital.

1. Friendly investors
2. Research and development tax shelters
3. Venture capitalists
4. Public offerings

FRIENDLY INVESTORS

Many software firms begin as a self-financed organization and then obtain the next round of financing by inviting friends and relatives to invest in the venture. Assuming that such invitations comply with state and federal legal requirements, the software entrepreneur can usually raise moderate sums ($20,000 to $50,000) from each friendly investor.

There are some obvious advantages to raising funding from such a group:

1. *Ease of funding.* Normally a friend or relative will not require extensive business plans or background research. Thus, if funds can be obtained from a friendly group, such an effort is usually easier.
2. *Speedy decisions.* This is tied into number 1. Not only is the funding easier to obtain, but the decision to invest is speedier. This eliminates some very difficult waiting periods.
3. *Supportive investors.* An entrepreneur must face the fact that all investors may not appreciate the entrepreneur's brilliance. Usually a friendly investor is more supportive than a total stranger.

There are also some negative aspects;

1. *The moral dilemma.* It is unclear whether it is morally proper to obtain investments from unsophisticated parties even if the entrepreneur believes the investment to be worthwhile. Such a dilemma leads the entrepreneur to some very difficult future decisions.
2. *The risk of loss.* Any venture can fail. It's destructive enough to the entrepreneur to have to face failure, let alone face former friends who have also lost money.
3. *The dry well.* Most ventures require several rounds of financing. Usually friends and relatives are not capable of extensive reinvestment. Thus the entrepreneur will have to expend additional effort to obtain funding.

Should you utilize friends and relatives for financing? There is no one answer, but you certainly should strongly consider the downside risk.

RESEARCH AND DEVELOPMENT TAX SHELTERS

With a research and development tax shelter plan, as with any investment plan, careful legal and financial drafting and construction are required. Unless the entrepreneur is an experienced tax attorney, CPA, and R & D tax shelter specialist, he or she should not attempt to construct such a transaction alone.

In concept, the structure of these transactions is relatively simple. A partnership puts up $X (and sometimes guarantees $Y in loans) for the development of a software product. The partnership issues a research and development (R & D) contract to the entrepreneur's firm for $X + $Y − $M (where $M is all administrative partnership costs including finders fees, legal expenses, and accounting costs). The partnership owns the results of the R & D contract and normally then licenses the technology to the software firm to market in return for royalties. The royalties may be a fixed amount, a fixed percentage, or a variable. The result of this transaction to the partnership is that they are able to write off as a deduction against ordinary income the $X + $Y in the year the funds were paid to the software firm. Additionally, they receive back royalties, which are usually taxed as long-term capital gains.

The advantages of such a transaction to the software entrepreneur are as follows:

1. Normally $200,000 to $500,000 can easily be raised to fund product development.
2. The royalty rates come out of sales; thus payments are deferred until the software product generates income.
3. The investment group normally maintains a very low profile, allowing the entrepreneur to run his or her business as necessary.

The disadvantages are:

1. The funding cannot be used for marketing expenses and the entrepreneur must still seek some investment capital for that effort.
2. The entrepreneur must negotiate a livable deal since if the royalty rate is too high the contribution of the product may be either negligible or negative.
3. There are a few professionals and a lot of wishful promoters in this area. Thus, when trying to obtain funding, the entrepreneur should be extremely careful in investing time with an unknown group.

The normal royalty is usually in the 20 to 35 percent range and this percentage can usually be decreased after a certain target has been achieved. It is not uncommon for finders feeds, legal expenses, and accounting charges to average 10 to 20 percent of the funding. Exactly who pays what to whom should be negotiated at a very early stage of the project.

VENTURE CAPITALISTS

There exist in the United States and abroad roughly 200 plus firms that specialize in investing in fledgling companies. Most of these groups prefer technologically oriented firms and most consider start-up investments. There is no general profile of a venture capitalist's deal. However, there are a few key ingredients:

- *Equity.* The venture capitalist ultimately wants equity in the firm. The percentage of equity varies but often the venture capitalist chooses to control the company via ownership of more than 50 percent of the voting stock. This percentage is negotiable, but it is a fact of life that the venture capitalist will own enough of the firm to participate on the Board of Directors and influence decisions.

- *Evaluation.* Most venture capitalists hire very bright analysts who are paid to evaluate opportunities. Thus a business plan is required and the evaluation takes time.

- *Specialties.* Each venture capital group has its particular specialties. Thus a firm specializing in printed circuit technology may neither wish to invest in nor be familiar with computer software efforts.

- *Loyalties.* There is an immense (and rightful) loyalty to existing investments. Normally a venture capitalist will not invest in two competitive firms.

- *Cooperation.* There is a great network of cooperating venture capitalists who continually participate with each other in deals. Once one of the network decides against an investment, it is very unlikely that others will decide for it.

There are some sound advantages to obtaining capital from a venture capitalist:

1. *Adequate financing.* Most deals provide sufficient capital to the entrepreneur to achieve a viable plan. Usually, if the entrepreneur makes that plan, the venture capitalists are prepared for additional capital infusions.

2. *Investment management.* Whether or not the venture capitalist takes an active roll in management of the firm, these investors do take an active role in positioning the firm for a return of equity. They can introduce the firm to excellent commercial and investment bankers.

3. *Confidence.* It does help to tell a client that XYZ and Associates is one of your principal investors. If that firm has confidence in the firm, shouldn't your prospect?

There are of course, negatives to such a source:

1. *Marriage rites.* Like it or not, you're choosing a bride (or groom). Usually though, there is no divorce. If you can't get along with your investors, they will likely get along without you, bringing in new management.

2. *Dilution.* As mentioned, the venture capitalist takes equity. The more equity you give up, the less you own. The reality of this is more of a psychological disadvantage than a financial one, since a smaller share of a valuable company is worth more than the entire share of a valueless company.

3. *Time and effort.* Venture capitalists may brag that they can commit millions immediately to a deal. However, in reality it is very unlikely that the time frame from the point of initial contact until total funding will be less than three or four months.

Venture capitalists have recently begun to appreciate software firms. They are a good source of funding for software entrepreneurs, particularly after some initial success.

PUBLIC OFFERINGS

Public offerings are not to be undertaken without expert legal advice. The practice of securities law is highly specialized and the malpractice insurance charges associated with that practice are among the highest for lawyers. However, it is useful to note the types of public offerings. There currently are four varieties, each identified by the applicable code or regulation section. These are S–1, S–2, S–18, and Regulation A.

An S–1 registration is the general procedure allowed by the SEC. There are extensive disclosure and reporting requirements required and most new software ventures prefer to utilize other forms of offerings if possible.

An S–2 offering requires greater than usual detail as to the use of the proceeds and the principals of the company. This is oriented toward start-ups and is unavailable to companies with no substantial sales or net income.

An S–18 is a newly offered form permitting raising moderate amounts (up to $5 million) with regional filings. There are restrictions as to the operating characteristics and mode of securities sales.

Regulation A offerings are offered under exemptions from complete regulations as to initial filings and approvals as well as subsequent reporting. Currently offerings are limited to $1.5 million in capital.

Again it should be emphasized that the entrepreneur must be cautious with a public offering. There are substantial civil and criminal liabilities associated with such offerings. *Get professional advice.*

A BUSINESS PLAN

Certainly venture capitalists and usually R & D tax shelters require a business plan. Not only is such a plan a necessity for obtaining capital, it is also a necessity for managing a venture.

There are two aspects to a business plan: (1) content, which we will detail; (2) presentation, which we will discuss briefly. We'll begin with what a business plan should contain.

The following is an outline and commentary of business plans.

I. *Management summary.* This is an optional section which should summarize the contents of the plan and highlight the salient positive aspects. The section is optional because most business plans are sent out with a cover letter serving the same function.

II. *Introduction.* The introduction must be very well written, stating a brief company history, purpose, market factors, and technological factors that make this venture a winner.

III. *Use of proceeds.* This includes a summary of funding required, backed up by details later in the plan.

IV. *Risk factors.* The better defense against having the plan discarded is an offense explaining what the risks of this venture are and what the company plans to do to overcome those risks. Normally areas of risk in a software effort are product development, competition, user acceptance, and financial management.

V. *Management.* This section describes the management structure and the management individuals. There should be a biographical sketch of each individual, oriented toward his or her achievements. It is usually worthwhile to discuss any possible negatives associated with the principals.

VI. *Operational plan.* This section explains how the company plans to operate. It includes:

A. A qualitative statement of activities
B. A business plan based on objectives with events and scheduled achievements including development, marketing, and sales activities
C. Sales forecasts with stated assumptions
D. Staff schedules and costing, with assumptions
E. Income projections with assumptions
F. Cash flow projections with assumptions

VII. *Appendices.* These describe products in more detail and also provide other technical background.

All forecasts and projections should be for five years. They are prepared by quarter or by month, usually the latter.

The business plan should be from 20 to 50 pages. It must be well-thought out and well-written. If you are uncomfortable with preparing your own plan, you might want to consider using a consultant to prepare it. Your financial advisor can usually assist you. If not, there are some consultants who, for a price, will prepare a plan. Another possibility is to work with a writer. The result must be good because, assuming you are able to get in the door, you will not likely get a chance to rewrite the plan.

The presentation itself should look professional. It does not need to be typeset, but clearly the entire plan, including financial projections, should be typed. Copies should be clear and on bond paper, bound in a notebook or with a cover. It's common business practice to number the copies and place some statement of proprietary rights on the plan.

The "better" approach to obtaining venture capital is to:

1. Obtain a list of venture capital firms. There are commercial directories, less expensive industry sources, and lists in current literature.

2. Personally contact a subset of that list introducing yourself and inviting yourself to send a business plan.

3. Send a business plan with a cover letter.

4. Follow the plan in approximately one week with a call or visit.
5. "Get the money."

A good business plan is a valid tool for raising venture capital. Proper presentation of such a plan is very important and also time-consuming. An excellent assist to software entrepreneurial fund raising is a flip chart presentation that follows the plan and summarizes it.

The following is a sample fictitious business plan:

A BUSINESS PLAN
FOR COURAGEOUS
PROGRAMS CORPORATION*

I. INTRODUCTION

Courageous Programs Corporation (CPC) is a California corporation incorporated on January 1, 1980, and currently is a start-up organization, having engaged in initial corporate formalities and some introductory operations. The company's mailing address in 3255 Sunset Boulevard, Suite 609, Los Angeles, California 90181. Its phone number is (213) 466–1515.

CPC will direct its resources to the development, maintenance, and marketing of much-needed supplemental/computer software to Fortune 1000 companies for their Distributed Data Processing (DDP) systems.

Because of the dramatic increase in performance/price ratios of both large- and small-scale data processing hardware systems, many businesses have ordered large quantities of low-cost satellite computer systems. These computers, when integrated into corporate communications networks, actually distribute processing power to the end user. The degree of usability of the remote site varies depending on the quality of software and the technical capabilities of the remote site.

Fortunately for CPC, the software required for this very complex operation has not kept pace with the hardware development. This lag in technology is well recognized

---

*The material contained herein is proprietary to Courageous Programs Corporation and may not be reproduced or disclosed to any third party without the explicit written consent of Courageous Programs Corporation.

throughout the industry. Even IBM is encouraging the entry of independent software vendors into this marketplace.

As detailed in this business plan, CPC intends to service a selected portion of this marketplace. That segment is the "IBM shop" utilizing one or more large central IBM processors with a remote collection of standard IBM DDP devices. The current large-scale domestic market size (as indicated by International Data Corporation) is 3,000 plus organizations. The specific above-mentioned segment is over 300 and growing rapidly, estimated to be 25 percent larger each year.

There currently is no known direct competition in this field, mainly because of the recent emergence of the technology. CPC's management believes that other existing software companies will want to enter this marketplace but will be severely handicapped for two reasons. First, most software companies will not be willing to make the one-million dollar plus start-up investment required. Second, IBM will soon be announcing major new large-scale computer technology (the H series) which will force most software vendors to reinvest major funds in their current packages to make them operate with the new major computer systems. This latter effort is nontrivial and will certainly delay any new development activities in additional technical arenas.

In summary, CPC plans to enter quickly a virgin yet rapidly expanding marketplace. The CPC organization brings considerable financial, marketing, sales, and technical expertise. The principals have worked together before and have a proven track record. This business opportunity is a significant one and has been well-researched by CPC. The above combined factors will greatly enhance CPC's probability of success.

II. USE OF PROCEEDS

CPC requires $1.4 million of start-up capitalization. This number is derived from a projected maximum cumulative cash deficit of ($1,019,000) in the ninth quarter of operation.

The plan developed by CPC's management is a conservative one. The staffing levels projected are based on exceptionally competent individuals working 60 plus hours per week to develop new software systems. However, the deliverables scheduled in the plan are achievable.

The approximate allocation of funds will be as follows:

1. Engineering costs $680,000
2. Marketing and sales costs $270,000
3. Administrative (including all $210,000
   facilities and support)

The categories are somewhat overlapping in that engineering will also provide marketing support as well as some of its own administrative support. The marketing costs actually include participation in development activities since CPC firmly believes that products must be keyed into the marketplace. Administrative costs overlap both groups in that administrative personnel will assist in sales activities as well as assist in development.

CPC prefers to obtain "vested" commitments for all required funding. There is no time available in this plan to obtain supplemental financing since all three principals will be heavily involved in start-up activities.

Additionally CPC will raise approximately $100,000 from its employees through stock option plans.

The founders of CPC welcome investor participation on the Board of Directors and, although insistent upon maintaining the day-to-day control of operations, are open to reasonable equity and/or debt financing arrangements.

III. RISK FACTORS

This is a start-up venture. Obviously there are inherent risks with any beginning organization. Additionally there are specific risks associated with the computer software market. Some of these risks are discussed in this section.

Product development. An essential component of CPC's success is on-time development of quality products. The three principals of CPC have over 40 years of cumulative experience in the computer industry. It is their belief that these development cycles are achievable. Additionally the unique concept of "contingent" royalties will encourage the development teams to meet the required schedules.

Product acquisition. CPC plans to acquire products from nonemployee authors (individuals or companies) in order to provide initial marketing impetus. We are confident of our success in this endeavor as one of the principals is a recognized industry authority on such transactions while the other two principals have packaged (i.e., cleaned up technically and prepared market materials) and introduced over eight software systems.

Competition. CPC must launch an aggressive sales campaign. CPC believes that in the future there may be competitive organizations with potentially similar product offerings. However, there currently is no company specializing in DDP operations-oriented software and it is CPC's opinion that the total approach taken in this plan will provide CPC with competitive advantages as well as a one- to two-year lead. Thus CPC will be able to be an industry leader placing competition in a catch-up role.

User acceptance. Any product must be accepted by the user community. In order to increase the likelihood of customer acceptance, CPC plans to utilize a sponsor site concept whereby several potential users assist in the design and testing of new products. This does not guarantee success but it does provide very valuable input.

Financial adequacy. The funds requested by CPC are its management's best projection of the investment required. These projections may have some variance. If they vary to the high side, CPC may choose to acquire one or more additional products from outside sources, thus being able to enter the marketplace more quickly. If they vary to the low side, CPC may be faced with raising additional capital or delaying some project implementations, CPC believes that future project funding would be available through research tax shelter programs. However, such funding would require substantial royalty payouts (25 to 35 percent) and would partially decrease profitability.

IV. MANAGEMENT

The three principals of CPC are John Doe, Jane Smith, and Jack Roe, who will serve as President, Senior Vice-President of Marketing and Sales, and Vice-President of Program Engineering. The following are abbreviated resumes of these individuals.

John Doe

John Doe was most recently Vice-President, Planning for Meek Systems, Inc. In that position he was responsible for corporate planning, product acquisition, and market research for Meek Systems. Additionally, he coordinated the nondomestic marketing activities and served as a member of the company's management committee while reporting directly to the chief executive officer. At Meek Systems, he acquired nine products, which constituted over one-third of the company's business. Mr. Doe began his career at Meek Systems as a sales representative and was always over quota.

Prior to Meek Systems, Mr. Doe was a marketing manager for Super Systems, Inc., where he sold proprietary software and directed professional services activities.

Prior to this activity Mr. Doe was a consultant, an analyst for Large Business Machines Corporation.

Mr. Doe received a B.S. and Master of Engineering from East Coast University, where he majored in Industrial Management and minored in Computer Science while working as a programmer and instructor in Data Processing.

Mr. Doe is 31 years old and married with 8 children.

Jane Smith

Jane Smith was most recently a consultant to a leading computer software company. Prior to that she was group manager of two Meek Systems divisions responsible for marketing, engineering, and customer support staffs. She served as Vice-President of Marketing for Meek Systems, recruiting sales and marketing personnel. Under Ms. Smith's direction this group generated over 40 percent of total domestic revenue. Ms. Smith developed sales and promotional strategies, introduced new products, and conducted product-oriented market research.

Prior to Meek Systems, Ms. Smith was one of four principals who founded the Commercial Software Division of Computers Inc. She personally defined marketing strategies, set pricing, and hired, trained, and managed the sales force for the central region.

Ms. Smith gained her initial data processing experience with XYZ, where she was a systems engineer.

Ms. Smith received a Bachelor of Science from the University of Clairol. Ms. Smith is 31 years old and unmarried.

Jack Roe

Jack Roe was the senior corporate technical consultant at Meek Systems, where he was in charge of evaluation of new software products, research of new IBM product offerings, and corporate technical audits. Prior to that position he was a senior software engineer who provided the project direction for Meek Systems' QUIET product. Mr. Roe redesigned and rewrote that package as well as serving as a senior consultant. He twice received the President's Engineering Award for Unobtrusive Performance.

Previously Mr. Roe was a Planning Analyst for Oil Glut, Inc., where he researched and evaluated hardware and software directions for the company. Before this he was a systems programmer who maintained and modified operating system software.

Mr. Roe was an honors graduate from the University of Ease with a Bachelor of Mathematics degree, having majored in applied analysis and computer science.

Mr. Roe is single and is 33 years old.

All three individuals were former employees of Meek Systems, Inc., and parted that organization on friendly terms. This business does not utilize any proprietary trade secrets of Meek Systems and CPC does not plan to raid Meek Systems for additional employees. Although Meek Systems will not welcome this venture with open arms because of its potential long-term competitive possibilities, CPC's founders are not aware of any fact that could lead to litigation by Meek Systems against CPC.

Other key personnel will be accepted after start-up funding. CPC sees no major problem in obtaining qualified staffing: the principals have extensive industry contacts, the company will provide state-of-the-art development projects, and the technical compensation (including deferred royalties) is most competitive.

V. GENERAL OPERATIONAL PLAN

A. Introduction

This business plan outlines CPC's entry into and penetration of the distributed data processing (DDP) software arena. The basis for this entry is a tie-in to IBM's DDP strategy and will be oriented toward IBM's larger customers (S/370 158's, 3032's, and above).

1. Rationale

The rationale for this approach is as follows:

- IBM, in spite of its late entry into DDP, is already setting the industry standard.
- Large IBM installations already are accustomed to purchasing non-IBM developed software and will require less sales education.
- Most large IBM user sites have sizable budgets for outside software procurement.

2. Approach

Since the IBM DDP market is expected to grow substantially, the two segments that are most suitable for penetration are the IBM 8100 and IBM 4300 series. Some existing software is already available for the 4300. However, no existing 8100 products are yet available from independent software vendors.

International Data Corporation (IDC) projects that 30 percent of the existing large systems marketplace currently has 8100's on firm order. This represents a prospect base of 360 sites (30% x 1200 U.S., MVS [i.e., larger] installations). The 4300 will likely achieve equal or greater penetration than the 8100.

In the 8100 marketplace, time is of the essence in order to get a jump on competition. Certain areas have been identified consistent with our initial study results. This analysis demonstrated that two initial offerings will provide excellent entry vehicles. These products are detailed in Appendix A. These are a DDP System Manager and a DDP Trend Analyzer. Thus the events to be completed are as follows:

- A short but complete 8100 external product design study.
- A detailed internal product design for the DDP system manager and for the DDP Trend Analyzer concurrent with a completed external design for the complete system offerings.
- A crash implementation for the DDP System Manager and for the DDP Trend Analyzer with concurrent detailed product design for the remainder of the initial offerings product line.
- An initial marketing program including launch of a sales campaign within one year from initiation of 8100 external product design.

The 4300 series marketplace will be attacked via use of adapted DOS/VSE and VM software. These packages will be acquired from outside sources, revised and marketed with royalty payments to the author.

B. Business Plan

The objectives of this business plan are:

- To achieve market presence within one year for the IBM 8100.
- To acquire a set of quality 4300 products and to market these within six months.
- To achieve 5 percent incremental customer penetration per year.
- To obtain repeat business from existing customers equal to or greater than the value of initial business in successive years.

1. Market Presence (8100)

In order to achieve 8100 market presence within one year, CPC will undertake two concurrent development projects.

The first of these—the DDP System Manager—will provide any DDP user with an inventory of physical equipment, software systems, network configuration, and user attributes. A data processing management staff would use this package to manage daily operations. Several user organizations have expressed a need for such a package. However, the real key to this product is that the information contained would be utilized by all of CPC's additional product offerings. This product is the base system to which additional product offerings will be interfaced, thus capitalizing on the technology and reducing future product development time. There is no similar product offering existing in the marketplace. Current research does not indicate near-term competitive availability.

The second project—the DDP Trend Analyzer—will be an essential ingredient in any user's plans. With this tool the user will be able to determine the history of use and what level of service is available from existing network configurations in order to alleviate the user work effort to obtain detailed rights.

The schedule for the first two projects is as follows:

Event	Completion Time
DDP System Manager System Design	Week 12
DDP Trend Analyzer System Design	Week 12
Identify two to five user sponsor sites	Week 13
DDP System Manager Internal Design	Week 16
DDP Trend Analyzer Internal Design	Week 18
DDP System Manager Program, Documentation and Test Plan	Week 28
DDP Trend Analyzer Program, Documentation and Test Plan	Week 30
Testing of DDP System Manager	Week 40
Announcement of DDP System Manager	Week 42
Testing of DDP Trend Analyzer	Week 44
Announcement of DDP Trend Analyzer	Week 50

2. 4300 Product Line

CPC will acquire two DDP-oriented products from nonemployee developers for the IBM 4300 series.

The normal mode of operation for such activities is that a nominal front end sum is advanced against royalties and the author receives royalties over a set period of time. The royalty rate usually varies from 15 to 50 percent and the period of time of royalty payments from five to seven years.

The type of product(s) to be acquired would be of a utility nature and would be likely candidates for rewrite to function on the 8100.

The schedule for these activities would be as follows:

Event	Completion Time
First advertisement for products	Week 1
Second advertisement for products	Week 3
Acquisition of product 1	Week 12
Acquisition of product 2	Week 14
Identification of two to five user sponsor sites	Week 15
Packaging of product 1	Week 16
Packaging of product 2	Week 18
Testing of product 1	Week 20
Testing of product 2	Week 22
Announcement of product 1	Week 24
Announcement of product 2	Week 28

3. Five Percent Incremental Customer Penetrations

As a conservative estimate, the existing qualified domestic marketplace is 360 sites. The growth rate of this marketplace is 10 percent annually. The European and Japanese marketplace is essentially equal to that in the United States (see Section D). An unofficial IBM source has stated that DDP shipments in Europe and Japan are greater than those in the United States.

The following table displays market size:

TABLE 1   MARKET SIZE FOR LARGE–SCALE DDP USERS

Year	Domestic Sites
1982	360
1983	396
1984	436
1985	480
1986	528
1987	581

Note that the above sites are Fortune 1000-like organizations. Their normal data processing budget is in the millions and often software expenditures approach a seven-digit number. It should be emphasized that the potential market size is 1,500 plus customers. Table 1 displays actual, qualified organizations.

In order to achieve a 5 percent incremental penetration, CPC must sell the following new customers per year:

TABLE 2   REQUIRED NEW
CUSTOMERS PER YEAR

Year	New Customers
1982	20
1983	22
1984	24
1985	26
1986	29
Total:	121

This plan is achievable in that it shows only a 7 percent penetration of the total market. Not all customers will buy all products. Many software organizations add 50 to 100 new customers per product per year. In CPC's case, this incremental approach plus the follow-on approach listed in Section B.4 provide for a conservative and achievable revenue base.

4. Market Program

In support of CPC's sales forecast, a directed and extensive marketing program is planned. CPC believes in the strength of a sound marketing program designed to maximize sales while concurrently holding related expenses to a minimum. Insofar as most of CPC's potential customers are readily identifiable, directed marketing programs will be implemented, as well as special programs designed to establish CPC as *the* leader in its field. The marketing programs will encompass several techniques.

(a) *Articles.* Here CPC will take advantage of the demand from publication editors for news material. The insertions are done at no charge (though at the discretion of each editor) and are known generally to receive wide readership and be viewed as credible. CPC will establish company credibility by having its employees submit technology trend articles relating to the industry it services. Additional articles will be written to establish CPC's product credibility. These will pertain to product introduction and user testimonials.

(b) *Advertisement.* CPC believes that a company that excludes itself from advertising in trade publications is rapidly forgotten by the industry. CPC intends to lead its field and be the major name in the user community. The initial theme of advertising will be to equate CPC with Distributed Data Processing software products. During the first year of operation, there will be little product advertising. Instead, ads will establish the company identity and capability.

(c) *Sponsor program.* The founders of CPC have previously experienced success in using a product sponsorship program. This involves selecting a small group of companies willing to acquire a new product in exchange for: a reduction in price; participation in designing the scope of the product; participation as a Beta Test Site; and additional technical "hand-holding" assistance. CPC will employ a sponsorship program, accepting a maximum of six sponsor companies. From these six sites CPC will also get its initial reference account base and user testimonial articles. (Note that marketing projections show four sponsors.)

(d) *Direct mail program.* Experience shows the success of direct mail campaigns for software products in generating interest and leads. Since the products will be developed and packaged in a manner designed to allow initiation of the sales cycle without personal sales visits, a direct mail campaign will be implemented to elicit response from highly qualified prospect companies. This concept will result in a greater number of qualified leads, while conserving costs.

(e) *Telephone campaign.* The telephone will be used judiciously to minimize the expense and time consumption of personal visits. While there will certainly be occasions when personal visits will be required during the sales cycle, the telephone will help make them as productive as possible. Besides utilizing the telephone for sales calls, CPC will use this medium for surveying user needs and wants. This is a unique application of this medium in the data processing industry and is expected to generate an excellent list of leads and product suggestions. It should be emphasized that our sales staff will be highly qualified and also directed in those techniques.

(f) *Sales information system.* Lead generation with poor follow-up is inexcusable. No known sales information and reporting system is available to assist in this area. The marketing program planned by CPC will be significantly enhanced by a system to track leads, analyze program effectiveness, relate expense of a program to revenue derived from that program, and so on. There is a need within all marketing-oriented companies for this type of function. Thus, for CPC's own requirement, we will develop a product that will be designed to be salable to other companies. This product will be added to CPC's product list or sold to a marketing company for cash and/or royalty fees. We believe that we can obtain a retainer to implement this system from an existing timesharing vendor.

CPC's marketing program is designed to generate leads of only the highest quality, thus allowing CPC to keep its sales staff to a minimum number of well-paid professionals. By eliminating as many garbage leads as possible, the sales staff can devote their energies toward closing business.

C. Market Forecasts—Domestic Operations

The following represents CPC's projections of domestic market activities. The assumptions utilized are:

1. Sales will initially be made to four sponsor sites at a 50 percent reduction in price.
2. All sales will include enhancement fees.

Product	Quarter 1	Quarter 2	Quarter 3		Quarter 4		Total	
(In house)								
DDP System Manager								
new	0	0	(2)	$20	(6)	$80	(8)	$100
enhancement	0	0		6		18		24
DDP Trend Analyzer								
new	0	0		0	(4)	20	(4)	20
enhancement	0	0		0		6		6
Host Batch Status								
new	0	0		0		0		0
enhancement	0	0		0		0		0
Product X								
new	0	0		0		0		0
enhancement	0	0		0		0		0
additional	0	0		0		0		0
maintenance	0	0		0		0		0
(Royalty)								
Action Services								
new	0	0		0	(4)	20	(4)	20
enhancement	0	0		0		6		6
additional	0	0		0		0		0
maintenance	0	0		0		0		0
Online Status								
new	0	0		0	(4)	14	(4)	14
enhancement	0	0		0		4		4
additional	0	0		0		0		0
maintenance	0	0		0		0		0
Remote Batch Status								
new	0	0		0		0		0
enhancement	0	0		0		0		0
additional	0	0		0		0		0
maintenance	0	0		0		0		0
4300 Utility A								
new	0	0	(6)	20	(6)	30	(12)	50
enhancement	0	0		3		3		6
additional	0	0		0		0		0
maintenance	0	0		0		0		0
4300 Utility B								
new	0	0	(6)	20	(6)	30	(12)	50
enhancement	0	0		3		3		6
additional	0	0		0		0		0
maintenance	0	0		0		0		0
TOTAL:	0	0	(14)	72	(30)	234	(44)	306

3. Fifty percent of the users will purchase additional product copies.

4. Maintenance and enhancement renewals will be at a 100 percent rate for five years.

D. Nondomestic Operations

CPC plans to launch European and Japanese marketing efforts during the third year of operation. This activity will be handled through two sets of overseas agents, one for the European Common Market countries and the other in Japan. One of the principals has, in his previous position, launched such activities and has managed and coordinated overseas agent sales activities. Another has prepared product training and support organizations for these activities.

1. Nondomestic Market Forecast

The nondomestic market forecasts are based on a 25 percent higher sales price and a 65 percent royalty payment to the agents, who will also provide customer maintenance and all administrative support. All enhancement fees and maintenance are paid to the agent. (This is a very conservative approach, and in all probability nondomestic revenues will be higher than forecast.) The product pricing in U.S. dollars for nondomestic operations is as follows:

NONDOMESTIC PRICING

Product	Initial CPU Price	Yearly Enhance- ment Fee for Initial CPU	Additional CPU Price	Yearly Maintenance Fee per Additional CPU
DDP System Manager	$25,000	all	N/A	all
DDP Trend Analyzer	$13,000	paid	N/A	paid
Action Services	$13,000	to	$3,000	to
Online Status Reporter	$ 9,000	agent	$2,000	agent
Host Batch Status Reporter	$13,000	"	N/A	"
Remote Batch Status Reporter	$ 7,000	"	$2,000	"
4300 Utility System A	$ 8,000	"	$3,000	"
4300 Utility System B	$ 8,000	"	$3,000	"

E. Staffing

The initial staffing will consist of the three principals with additional development engineers, product managers, secretaries, a secretary/bookkeeper, and one technical secretary phased in as required.

1. Staff Allocation

The staffing by quarter with direct salaries is as follows:

STAFFING COURAGEOUS PROGRAMS CORPORATION (SAMPLE)
(000's omitted)

Position	Qt. 1	Qt. 2	Qt. 3	Qt. 4	Qt. 5	Qt. 6	Qt. 7	Qt. 8	Qt. 9	Qt. 10	Qt. 11	Qt. 12
A	12	12	12	12	13	13	13	13	14	14	14	14
B	12	12	12	12	13	13	13	13	14	14	14	14
C	12	12	12	12	13	13	13	13	14	14	14	14
Sr. Eng.	0	10	10	10	10	12	12	12	12	13	13	13
Eng. 1	0	0	0	9	9	9	9	10	10	10	10	11
Eng. 2	0	0	0	0	9	9	9	9	10	10	10	10
Eng. 3	0	0	0	0	0	9	9	9	9	10	10	10
Eng. 4	0	0	0	0	0	9	9	9	9	10	10	10
Eng. 5	0	0	0	0	0	9	9	9	9	10	10	10
Eng. 6	0	0	0	0	0	0	9	9	9	9	10	10
Prod. mgr.	0	0	0	0	0	9	9	10	10	10	10	11
Sales 1	0	0	0	0	18	18	18	18	21	21	21	21
Sales 2	0	0	0	0	0	18	18	18	18	21	21	21
Sales 3	0	0	0	0	0	0	18	18	18	18	21	21
Sales 4	0	0	0	0	0	0	0	18	18	18	18	21
Sales 5	0	0	0	0	0	0	0	0	18	18	18	18
Sales 6	0	0	0	0	0	0	0	0	18	18	18	18
Sales 7	0	0	0	0	0	0	0	0	0	18	18	18
Secy/bkr.	4	4	4	4	5	5	5	5	5	5	6	6
Tech. secy.	0	0	0	4	4	4	4	5	5	5	5	6
Sales secy.	0	0	0	0	0	0	4	4	4	4	5	5
Controller	0	0	0	0	0	0	0	0	7	7	7	7
Sales coordin.	0	0	0	0	0	0	0	0	0	13	13	13
Total	40	50	50	63	94	150	181	202	255	293	299	309

F. Estimated Income Statement

The following statement is based on these assumptions.

1. New product sales—domestic as indicated in Section C.
2. New product sales—nondomestic as indicated in Section D.
3. Royalties at 20 percent with direct payments to nonemployee authors. Employees receive deferred compensation based on royalty payments on a project-by-project basis with vesting only after CPC profitability and five years of employment.
4. Direct personnel as indicated in Section E.
5. Indirect personnel costs (insurance, FICA, SDI) at 30 percent of direct.
6. Office expenses based on start-up facilities.
7. Phone and postage as a nondirect function of marketing activities.
8. Promotion expenses are shown when incurred.
9. Furniture and supplies as a nondirect function of personnel.
10. Computer costs estimated at high level. Costs may be reduced either through equipment acquisition or trades.
11. Travel and entertainment as a function of marketing activity with an additional allowance for nondomestic operations.
12. Legal and accounting showing year-end surges.

COURAGEOUS PROGRAMS CORPORATION
PROJECTED INCOME STATEMENT
(000's omitted)

	Year 1	Year 2	Year 3	Year 4	Year 5
SALES INCOME					
Domestic	$306	$1853	$2979	$4123	$5034
Nondomestic	0	0	596	1137	1394
Total: Sales	$306	$1853	$3575	$5260	$6428
Less: Royalties	61	371	715	1052	1286
Net Income	$245	$1482	$2860	$4208	$5142
EXPENSES					
Direct personnel	$203	$627	$1152	$1320	$1480
Indirect personnel	61	188	357	404	444
Office	14	26	40	56	64
Phone & postage	40	55	72	60	80
Promotion	70	90	120	140	200
Computer	60	110	140	140	160
Travel & entertainment	85	60	80	100	120
Legal & accounting	16	19	21	24	24
Furniture & supplies	19	13	16	20	24
Total Expenses	$568	$1188	$1998	$2264	$2596
Profit	(−$323)	$294	$862	$1944	$2546
Profit after tax	(−$323)	$294	$431	$972	$1273

G. Cash Flow

CPC has prepared a cash flow projection, based on the following assumptions:

1. Domestic revenue received one quarter after billings.
2. Nondomestic revenue not recorded until payment received by agent, and revenue received by CPC one quarter later.
3. Royalties at 20% with direct payments to nonemployee authors. Employees receive deferred compensation based on royalty payments on a project-by-project basis with vesting only after CPC profitability and five years of employment.
4. Direct personnel costs as indicated in Section E.
5. Indirect personnel costs (insurance, FICA, SDI) at 30 percent of direct.
6. Office expenses based on start-up facilities.
7. Phone and postage as a nondirect function of marketing activity.
8. Furniture and supplies as a nondirect function of personnel.
9. Computer costs estimated at high level. Costs may be reduced either through equipment acquisition or trades.
10. Travel and entertainment as a function of marketing activity with an additional allowance for nondomestic operations.
11. Legal and accounting showing year-end surges.
12. Taxes as indicated.

COURAGEOUS PROGRAMS CORPORATION CASH FLOW PROJECTIONS (SAMPLE)
Year One (000's omitted)

	Quarter 1	Quarter 2	Quarter 3	Quarter 4
Sales income				
Domestic	0	0	0	72
Nondomestic	0	0	0	0
Total sales	0	0	0	72
Less: royalties	0	75	0	0
Net income	0	(75)	0	72
Expenses				
Direct personnel	40	50	50	63
Indirect personnel	12	15	15	19
Office	5	3	3	3
Phone & postage	10	10	10	10
Promotion	20	15	15	20
Computer	10	10	20	20
Travel & entertainment	25	20	20	20
Legal & accounting	10	2	2	2
Taxes	2	0	0	0
Furniture & supplies	10	3	3	3
Total expenses	144	128	138	160
Cash flow	(144)	(203)	(138)	(88)
Cumulative cash flow	(144)	(347)	(485)	(573)

APPENDIX: PRODUCT DESCRIPTION SUMMARY

CPC plans to implement the following family consisting of at least six 8100 network products. These will supplement two DOS/VSE 4300 utilities, to be acquired from outside authors, and to be converted to 8100 use if appropriate. The basic six products will be:

- *8100 System Network Manager.* This is CPC's flagship product serving as a computer network inventory/manager by maintaining records of all hardware, software, and users with appropriate attributes. This system will maintain the data base of configuration characteristics which will be used by CPC's other products.
- *8100 Trend Analyzer.* This product will analyze data from IBM's standard PT (performance tool) and report on exception conditions and performance trends.
- *8100 Action Services.* The Action Services programs will allow the analyst to alter system parameters to eliminate problems. The action sources system will be utilized in conjunction with the 8100 Online Status.
- *8100 Online Status.* This system will display network operational characteristics as well as localized 8100 information. It will provide "alarm" capabilities once a threshold is exceeded.
- *Host Batch Status.* The Host Batch Status system will collect information regarding the network (including 4300's, 8100's, etc.) associated with a large CPU and will then be able periodically to report overall statistics.
- *Product X.* This will either be a network capacity planner or a network security system. After initial product launch, CPC will decide whether these products justify development funding based on a thorough product evaluation analysis.

8100 Systems Network Manager

The 8100 Systems Network Manager is CPC's flagship product and will be installed at a large percentage of our customer sites. It performs two basic functions:

1. *Systems inventory control.* By maintaining a record of all hardware, licensed software in the network, and users along with pertinent attributes, a manager will be able to administer the system.
2. *Data attribute management.* The network manager will enable CPC to utilize information contained therein with other software systems.

There is a pressing need for a computer system inventory management function. This product is adaptable in that it will create a market with users who have not yet installed DDP networks. Most prospect sites have multiple vendors providing hardware and software. This is a major management problem, particularly in light of the fact that networks will scatter sites and multiple software copies. The Systems Network Manager maintains records of all products installed at a corporation and reports on lease expirations, maintenance renewals, and other pertinent financial information. In addition, it will be a convenient repository for configuration and user data, allowing online display of the hardware and software available at a particular site or throughout the entire network. The data attribute management function will prevent duplication of these efforts with other CPC products. Because of this economy of function, the user is encouraged to use several CPC products. This factor provides a resiliency to the competition that will eventually develop in the market.

8100 Trend Analyzer

This is CPC's initial "performance" product. On the basis of our industry experience, we believe the analyst needs to have concise reporting rather than being presented with complicated, voluminous reports. This system will report summary data as well as certain exceptional or unusual conditions. It will also be capable of adding attribute information to the 8100 Systems Network Manager data attribute management facility. This enables the reporting of predictive future leads. Additionally, the Trend Analyzer could be tied into a Network Capacity Analyzer product.

The 8100 Trend Analyzer will obtain data from IBM's 8100 Performance Tool, an IBM-licensed and -supported product. Using this IBM facility to gather data will insulate the Trend Analyzer from 8100 operating system changes and thus considerably reduce maintenance. On the basis of our experience in the performance industry, CPC's principals believe that the user would prefer extensive reporting with no operating system dependencies.

8100 Action Services

The 8100 Action Services product allows an analyst to modify system parameters to expedite processing and to eliminate problems. This product allows the analyst much greater control over the operation of the system and will enable the analyst to avoid having to restart the computer hardware, which is a very troublesome function in an on-line system.

This product will tie into the 8100 Online Status product in order to allow the analyst to monitor the status of tasks in the 8100.

This type of product has proven very successful for larger systems and will be very well accepted for 8100 users.

8100 Online Status

The 8100 Online Status product is designed to provide an 8100 "node" with information regarding the activity of a specific 8100.

The product will display on a CRT formatted information regarding the work being done on an 8100. It will allow threshold limits to be set and notice to be provided to an analyst. This is, in essence, an alarm.

Additionally, this product will feed into the Host Batch Status program.

Host Batch Status

The Host Batch Status system will collect information from various network nodes as well as from the local network control programs to provide very detailed information regarding network activities.

The user will utilize this sytem to determine activity on the teleprocessing network as well as allowing the user to concentrate on service levels to a given individual.

This system interfaces with the 8100 Online Status utilities to provide detailed local and remote information. It will also allow a user to maintain precise data for projections of future needs.

Additional Product Possibilities

- *Network Capacity Planner.* This system will provide modeling as a capacity planner. It will use analytic modeling (i.e., network queuing theory) techniques to produce a model of the analyst's existing or proposed networks.

  Once an analyst sets up models, he or she can predict the effect of new hardware and applications added to the existing network.

  CPC would likely seek assistance from academic professionals to design the queuing model.

- *Network Security System.* The Network Security System maintains profiles of all authorized users of the system and validates a user's authority when he or she begins to use the system. A security "officer" would be able to maintain the security operations. The system would maintain access records as occurring.

  The product would tie into IBM-provided systems and thus would be economically maintained.

Appendix B

LEGAL PROTECTION
OF SOFTWARE

Since the most valuable asset of a new software entrepreneurial venture is the first software product, it is very important to protect the system from legal misuse. The entrepreneur, with the aid of legal counsel, should prepare a detailed set of policies and procedures to enhance this protection.

Although the materials presented in this Appendix are reasonably comprehensive, it is intended only as an introduction to this area. Be certain to discuss these concepts with your attorney. If, after reading this section, you know more than your current attorney, find a new one!

We have already mentioned that software is treated as a special kind of property, i.e., intellectual property. The U.S. legal system provides three basic forms of protection for intellectual property: patents, copyrights, and trade secrecy agreements. Before examining each of these, we should first discuss the term, "legal protection." Assume that someone, a villain, in some manner takes your software product and either uses it without paying for it or, even worse, begins to sell it without your permission. You want to stop the villain's activity and recover any damages such as lost profit or diminished reputation. In essence, you want a court to issue an order prohibiting the villain from using or distributing your product and to award you a judgment from the villain for the damages suffered by you.

There is currently a controversy over how to protect software. Most legal experts agree that it is a form of intellectual property similar to inventions or works of art. However, beyond that point there is no unanimous view as to which of the three methods of protection to use to get relief. This Appendix will not resolve that dispute. However, we will recommend some steps.

One of the most publicized methods of protection is a patent. The patent grants to the developer/inventor the ability to prohibit others from using a patented program without paying a royalty. Unfortunately, as of now there is no definitive reading as to the patentability of computer programs. Recent U.S. Supreme Court decisions have upheld patents where a program was part of an industrial process. At this point, it seems that a program *plus* something is patentable. That "plus" is still subject to interpretation. This, coupled with the costly and involved patent process, means simply that patents are not the current preferred method of protection for a software product. However, this is a changing area and the entrepreneur should attempt to stay current on any new decisions.

The second method, which has evolved into favor because of recent changes in the law, is the copyright. The copyright gives the developer a right to prevent someone from copying his or her program provided that it has been published and marked with a copyright notice. Most newly written software systems from certain major companies are copyrighted and appropriate federal procedures are followed. At the very least, it is considered good practice to display the copyright notice properly. One major difficulty with the copyright is that Congress has yet been unable to draft complete laws that extend copyright protection from the original source code to corrected or modified versions of the product. This means that for every change, new copyright applications may be required. Additionally, there is a minority view of practicing computer lawyers that when Congress agreed to provide copyright protection to software, they prohibited other forms of protection. With the current backlog of legal issues to be decided in the court system, it will probably be well into the mid-1980's before some of this confusion is clarified. Even so, the software entrepreneur should certainly consider the use of a copyright to protect the software product.

The courts have also permitted individuals to protect valuable secrets by adhering to certain rules. This process is normally referred to as "trade secrets." The original concept was that someone should not unfairly misappropriate the know-how of another. Courts, concerned with fairness, established a body of law related to such trade secrets. This law is the creation of courts and not legislature; as such it varies from state to state. In general, if someone uses your program without permission, you must show that it is a trade secret *and* that someone obtained the secret by breach of a special relationship. For example, if you distribute your program to anyone without requiring the party to sign an agreement stating that it is a trade secret, you probably do not have that "special relationship" and, therefore will not be able to enforce the trade secrecy provision. The trade secret laws have been created to help a company enforce the trust put into special groups such as licensees of the product or employees who agree to develop systems. Normally the license or employment agreement will contain a very precise definition of trade secrecy and indicate the confidential and proprietary nature of the product.

As a practical matter, there are some customers who will never agree to your protection clauses. There is no magic way to get them to agree. You should try to rewrite the clause with them to get the necessary effect. If you still cannot get what you want, you should face the fact that you may have to give up business to keep the protection that you want.

There is, then, no one way to protect systems. In fact, the best way might be a physical scheme of date-oriented releases which destroy themselves after a certain date. Another method might be to require the use of special hardware or firmware. Still another way might be to provide only certain key modules in such a way as to guarantee their technical obsolesence. Even with these protections, it is suggested that the entrepreneur develop the following policies:

1. Require employees to sign trade secrecy agreements.
2. Prohibit product use or distribution without the recipient's signing trade secrecy agreements.
3. Be certain that physical steps are taken to protect the code at the company site and at service bureaus.
4. Place copyright notices as required on the first screen, on the first report, on the computer tape, and anywhere else you believe is appropriate.
5. File copyright applications as required.

As a final note, this is a highly volatile area of computer law and the entrepreneur should be certain to review company practices with legal counsel. It is an excellent idea to have a second opinion. The greatest way to destroy something of value is to let it be distributed without charge.

BUSINESS FUNDAMENTALS

An individual who is not financially trained can usually learn a few basic fundamentals to assist in the financial management of the business. As with major tax and legal issues, the best source of information and assistance is a professional. Because of some of the unique issues associated with computer software, the entrepreneur is usually best with a financial advisor who is computer oriented.

What types of financial advisors are there? First, there is the CPA or certified public accountant. All CPA's have undergone testing and work requirement experience which allows them to certify audited financial statements. There are two general types of financial statements—audited and unaudited. A statement is considered to be audited after a CPA has reviewed the company's business records, tested the validity of those records, and then certified the results subject to numerous qualifications or footnotes. Only a CPA may provide this service. Additionally, a CPA can usually prepare tax returns, set up the company's accounting system, and offer general financial consulting.

The second type of professional is a public accountant, who normally has the requisite accounting education and has not chosen to become a CPA. There are many competent public accountants and, short of audited financial statements, they are able to provide most services needed by an entrepreneur.

The third type of advisor is a bookkeeper, who normally has some training in how to maintain the accounting information associated with the business. A good bookkeeper can not only provide excellent financial reports but also minimize outside accounting expenses. Many entrepreneurs hire part-time bookkeepers or hire a combination secretary/bookkeeper.

There is no magic formula as to which of these three types of individuals to use. In the usual situation, a firm starts with a bookkeeper and/or a public accountant and goes to a CPA only when the need for an audited statement arises. (Some banks and many outside investors require such an audited statement. Almost any form of public debt or equity offering absolutely necessitates an audited statement.)

Some entrepreneurs with an eye to the future begin with a CPA firm, which in turn recommends a bookkeeper or trains an employee of that firm. CPA firms are of various sizes with all the concomitant advantages and disadvantages. If you choose to work with a CPA firm, it is normally a good idea to have a law firm and CPA who know each other and who can work together.

There is also the fourth alternative available to an entrepreneur, and that is for the entrepreneur to serve as his or her own financial advisor. The new entrepreneur is urged to not consider this alternative on a first business venture. The risk associated with financial management is too great. With this warning in mind, we will now examine four fundamental financial management areas: cash, profit, tax, and equity.

CASH MANAGEMENT

The major reason for new business failure is insufficient cash to carry on the business. A well-done business plan carefully estimates cash needs. Even if these cash needs are met, a firm must initiate a cash management scheme.

Most financial advisors will implement their own methodology. The following is a suggested outline of a methodology with commentary on potential techniques.

Like any activity, cash management requires a plan. This plan is really short-term or tactical in nature. Normally a 90-day plan is done with monthly revisions. There are two major sections, the first dealing with cash sources and the second with cash requirements.

There are several sources of cash. At the beginning of any planning period there is usually cash available in the form of bank balances. Additionally, some cash may be expected from customers. The usual model for such activity is that a customer contracts for a software product, the product is shipped, and the client is billed for the product upon acceptance (which in some cases is the date of installation and in others is some specified time after delivery). The industry standard seems to be not to offer a discount for prompt payment although this is a feasible way to encourage customers to pay their bills. The payment cycles in most companies vary from immediate to several months. Since most start-up software companies are cash poor, the entrepreneurs frequently find themselves phoning the customer to encourage payment.

The cash source portion of the plan will attempt to conservatively estimate when payments will be received. It will normally be in the format shown in Figure C.1

Of note is the potential for a start-up company to borrow money from a bank. In spite of bank loan policies, which normally favor established companies, start-up organizations do have the ability to borrow funds on the basis of either their own activities, their receivables, or personal guarantees on the part of the entrepreneur. Poli-

Cash Sources	January	February	March
Bank accounts	$10,000		
Customer payments			
ABC, Inc.	7,600		
DEF Corp.	800	$800	$800
GHI Corp.		7,600	
JKL, Inc.			7,600
Other sources			
Bank loan		5,000	

FIGURE C-1   Cash plan

cies differ greatly from one bank to another and, where branch banking is available, from one branch to another. A competent entrepreneur will seek out a banking relationship that can provide some financing. In some cases, smaller banks may aggressively seek start-up companies with the hope that they will grow to be major clients. In other cases, larger banks may be more willing to risk a loan with a start-up firm. The real key here is the establishment of a good working relationship with a banker. Sometimes the company's legal or accounting firms can be of assistance. In general, the entrepreneur should initiate this relationship at a very early stage in the business, *before* the money is needed.

The cash requirements section is prepared by outlining fixed monthly expenditures and then proceeding to list variable expenditures when payment is anticipated. The start-up company is usually faced with a dilemma. In some ways, it is to the advantage of the entrepreneur to delay payments until absolutely necessary to preserve cash. In other ways it is exceptionally important to pay bills promptly to establish a favorable credit history. Usually, the operational mode is one of prompt payment of bills but minimization of variable cash expenses. Thus the entrepreneur, unless blessed

Cash Requirements	January	February	March
Fixed Expenses			
Salaries	$1,200	$1,200	$1,200
Taxes	250	250	1,000
Office rental	300	300	300
	$1,750	$1,750	$2,500
Variable Expenses			
Travel & Entertainment	$500	$300	$450
Advertising	0	0	500
Computer time	600	400	450
Equipment	100	100	150
Telephone	500	560	400
Other	650	350	1,400
	$2,350	$1,710	$3,350

FIGURE C-2   Sample cash requirements

with large cash balances, normally rents or leases capital equipment so as to minimize the impact of these expenditures. The cash requirements section would appear as in Figure C.2.

The example reflects a favorable cash position, but most start-up companies find such a favorable position to be a rarity and thus must expedite customer payments and delay bill paying so as to survive. Many an entrepreneur has lost sleep over how to meet this month's payroll. This is not an unusual problem, if any comfort can be found in knowing that you are not alone.

The major item to remember about cash management is that it must be done. To ignore cash management is to court financial disaster. More than one "profitable" software company has gone under for inability to meet its cash requirements.

PROFIT MANAGEMENT

Cash management is a survival technique. Profit management is a prerequisite to growth. There are two fundamental accounting systems or methods available which are used to determine accounting profit. The first is cash and the second is accrual.

A cash-based accounting system recognizes all income when it is received and all expenses when they are paid. An accrual accounting system recognizes all income when such income becomes due to the company and all expenses when they are incurred.

Most software companies operate on an accrual basis since this may present a truer picture of the company's financial status. Some companies keep a cash-basis picture for tax purposes with an accrual basis for management purposes.

The net effect of a cash-basis accounting system is to defer the receipt of income. Since the usual methodology is to treat all research and development effort as expenses, the difference of cash and accrual accounting as to expenses is minimized. Thus an ongoing growing company can defer taxes due by using a cash-basis accounting.

If cash-basis accounting is used, the income statement may be less reflective of the company's financial status. Thus normally management requires a picture of expenses due as well as income due. The entrepreneur should consult with a financial advisor to choose a method.

In either case, the entrepreneur is faced with a decision as to profit management. We have already seen in Chapter 16 how certain increases in allowable expenses and salaries can maximize income available. This is usually done at the expense of minimizing accounting profit.

The major disadvantage to minimizing accounting profit is that most bankers and investors like to see a history of profit and thus the entrepreneur may wish to manage financial operations to show an increasingly profitable operation. The entire question of profit management is very much tied into the entrepreneur's plans for the business. A desire to expand the business and thus perhaps go through a public offering requires a profit history.

TAX MANAGEMENT

All businesses require a tax management scheme. Normally any successful entrepreneur will minimize taxes due within legal limits. A tax/financial advisor will provide valuable advice to the company in tax management concepts.

Even unprofitable companies require tax management. Almost every financial decision carries with it tax consequences. For example, the decision to purchase equipment as opposed to renting or leasing it changes the tax implications. There are two fundamental tax concepts associated with capital equipment. The first deals with an investment tax credit. In order to encourage expansion, the tax laws offer certain incentives for purchasing of equipment in the form of a credit as a percentage of the capital cost. Second, capital equipment is usually depreciated (written off) over its life and several forms of depreciation are available. Since tax laws change almost yearly in this area, the entrepreneur should consult with tax advisors prior to any decision making.

One final note as to tax management. The payment of taxes (income, employee withholding, social security, and others) is an absolute necessity. Delinquencies are not tolerated and more than one software firm has rapidly failed after the government assessed a tax lien against the company (and in some cases padlocked the door). The IRS is probably the most powerful legal collection force in the world, as well as the most unsympathetic. One can strive to minimize taxes; however, one should not hope to avoid payment when taxes are due.

EQUITY MANAGEMENT

Equity not only represents value but also represents control. In spite of assurances to the contrary, an entrepreneur can lose control of his or her enterprise if someone or some group owns sufficient equity to oust the entrepreneur.

In general, the entrepreneur should guard against giving up equity unless necessary. This is not to say that some ownership may not be given to key employees or investors. However, the decision to give up equity is an important one. Just as borrowing money and the repayment of those borrowings can severely impact the entrepreneur, so can equity distribution.

There is no general rule of thumb. Many very successful entrepreneurs have given up large portions (greater than 50 percent) of their equity to finance growth. Others have maintained control throughout the life of the company. In either case, the entrepreneur should get to know any investors prior to investment. Most sophisticated venture capital groups do not want to step into management; most reasonable investors do not need to manage the companies in which they invest. On the other hand, some investors want to legally take over companies prior to any investment. Equity planning is a very important part of any company's activities.

Appendix D

SEMINAR KIT

ORGANIZATION

This kit is divided into a scheduled organization approach and is based on the premise that you will have 60 days to plan. You can do it in less time, but you are urged to allow the full 60 days.

HOW TO PREPARE FOR AND GIVE A SEMINAR

The principal aspect of seminar presentation is that the seminar must be well organized. In order to be well organized, it must be scheduled.

Sixty Days Prior to the Seminar

It is very important to set goals for a seminar. For example, one might wish to achieve $100,000 in sales from product revenues. The next step is to back-cut these goals. For example, the $100,000 in sales may mean five $20,000 sales, which in turn require at least ten prospects, which in turn mean 50 suspects must be invited.

The next step is to determine how to achieve these goals. Many good software seminar pitch men emphasize creating a need, since a need will stay with the attendees longer than the product knowledge imparted at the seminar. There are numerous tactics required to create a need:

1. Instill fear of the unknown.
2. Instill fear of a hardware vendor.
3. Instill fear of upper corporate management disapproval.
4. Show how knowledge can be gained from the product.
5. Tell "war stories" of product use.
6. Use users to convey the use of the product.

The seminar should be based on a list of cold, lukewarm, and warm prospects. The sources will include correspondence files, phone records, industry knowledge, current prospects, and published lists. You may wish to key reply cards to determine the sources.

Normally seminars are held in hotels. The best location might be at the airport, if that is centrally located. Free parking is an advantage. A high-quality hotel is usually preferable since the banquet costs are normally the same yet the staff and facilities are better. A good hotel staff is a necessity. In choosing a room, make an estimate and add 50 percent. You can usually obtain a larger room much more easily than a smaller one. Be certain to arrange for a registration table, display tables, audiovisual equipment, and refreshments. Choose a separate room for lunch. Personally visit the hotel and talk with the staff; then confirm all the arrangements by mail.

If you are using extra speakers, be certain to confirm their participation. The entrepreneur is usually the key speaker.

If you are going to have users speak, tell them what to say and be very careful. It's usually a given that unless you rehearse guest speakers they will probably embarrass you.

Create a tentative seminar schedule. Begin with coffee, milk, orange juice, and pastry. A schedule usually includes a welcome, a coffee break, lunch, a collection of seminar forms, a break, and a wrap-up. The actual presentation should be planned so that each event fits into a convenient break point.

Order printed material in a quantity greater than you expect to use. Normally you will require:

1. Letters of invitation
2. Return/reply cards
3. Product summaries
4. Confirmation letters (initial and follow-up)
5. Charts
6. Postage reply cards

Forty-Five Days Prior to the Seminar

You should now firm up the time schedule, develop a rough set of foils, and confirm the speakers. You should send out the invitations with reply cards, keeping returned letters to revise your records.

At the hotel you should set up the menu. Avoid alcohol at a light lunch if you want to keep your audience awake. Arrange for audiovisuals, including at least *two* black-boards, a speaker podium with a microphone, a screen, a slide and/or foil projector, and display stands. Be certain to request listings at the hotel.

If others are going to assist, present them with an outline. Confirm everything.

Thirty Days Prior to the Seminar

Now is the time to pack the house. Send out at least twenty personal invitations, including those to whom you have outstanding proposals and a few good friends.

If you are using overhead foils, be certain they are of good quality. You should also send out the initial confirmations of those responding and maintain copies of all replies. Be certain to have sufficient handouts as well as business cards.

It's advisable to use cue cards for the speakers stating:

1. SMILE
2. LOUDER
3. SPEED UP
4. SLOW UP
5. 15, 10, 5 MINUTES LEFT.

If you're giving the seminar, have someone else handle these cards.

Fifteen Days Prior to the Seminar

Reconfirm each responding individual's appointment, and if you still have space, mention that there is space available and ask the attendees to invite other associates.

Now is the time to reconfirm everything with the hotel. Ask them for a written reconfirmation. If you are having other participants, meet with them and rehearse.

Seven Days Prior to the Seminar

Rehearse and do a dry run.

Three Days Prior to the Seminar

Reconfirm all attendees via telephone. If they aren't coming, try to get someone else from the organization.

Talk again with the hotel and determine who will be available to meet you at 7 A.M. the day of the seminar.

Prepare name labels, which are to be sorted out manually.

One Day Prior to the Seminar

Prepare your supplies to include:

1. Tablets
2. Pencils
3. Chalk and holders
4. Erasers
5. Staples
6. Two pointers
7. Marking tape
8. Yellow markers
9. Scissors
10. Paper clips
11. Extra name tags
12. Felt tip pens
13. Aspirin
14. Cough drops
15. Handouts
16. Presentation copies
17. Business cards
18. Seminar forms
19. Reply cards

Confirm that your speakers are still alive and well.

Seminar Day

Get to the hotel early. Be certain the event board is set up with the seminar name. Find a hotel worker and tip him $10 to help you set up the seminar.

Be certain the room is set up with the proper number of chairs, a podium and mike, an overhead projector with a spare bulb, two blackboards, display stands, registration and display tables, and water, glasses, and ash trays.

Determine how to use the lights and manuals. Your handouts are optional. Normally you include a business card. Call the hotel catering department to confirm the times of meals and refreshments.

At registration have the tags and a sign-in form ready. Be certain to get people to register prior to getting coffee.

For the seminar try to set a friendly atmosphere and give the attendees an idea of the schedule. Normally one wishes to create a need, show the problems, and show simple reasons. Try to give a corporate overview showing strength, organization, and some futures.

At a wrap-up be certain to commit to contact and thank the attendees.

One Day After the Seminar

Send out personal thank yous with calls to urgent needs. Organize the attendees' seminar forms in order of priority and call all of them; then send another letter. The seminar form includes:

1. Name and title
2. Phone number
3. Address
4. Comments
5. Immediate need
6. Space for additional contacts

Appendix E

A LARGE SOFTWARE COMPANY'S VIEW OF THE SOFTWARE ENTREPRENEUR

This Appendix is a summary of an interview with Mr. Bruce T. Coleman, Executive Vice-President, Informatics, Inc. At Informatics, Mr. Coleman was previously group vice-president of Software Products, and, prior to his coming to Informatics, he was president of Boole & Babbage, Inc. Mr. Coleman holds an MBA from Harvard Business School, originally entered the computer field with IBM, and has been an active participant in ADAPSO. The views expressed in this Appendix are Mr. Coleman's and are not reflective of official Informatics's policy.

A large company views a software entrepreneurial venture in a different way from almost any other business venture. To the large company, software entrepreneurs represent sources of new products which can be offered through the large company's organization. There is no definitive study, but it is estimated that between 25 and 75 percent of all product offerings from large software companies are acquired from either software entrepreneurs or user organizations. Thus if a large software firm wishes to add two new products per year, the odds are very high that one of those products will be from an outside source, and very likely a software entrepreneur.

When a large software firm views a software entrepreneur, it does so with five major factors in mind: economics, motivation, the iceberg phenomenon, marketing and sales, and distribution. We will examine each of these areas.

The economics of a large software firm are rather straightforward. Typically, for a large firm of $10 million of sales per year, approximately 25 percent of sales revenue is invested in technology, 40 percent in sales and marketing, and 15 percent in administrative support. A smaller organization may not initially have this cost allocation. The significant point of this economic model is that if a software firm acquires a new product, the royalties over a five-year period must be less than 20 percent. These royalties may at first appear small to the entrepreneur, but they are a function of over-all sales. Often the total royalties paid may approach $1 million. There is no standard arrangement. However, there often is a sliding scale with higher initial fees decreasing over time. (Author's note: There are instances of higher royalty payments than suggested here. Often the royalty is sweetened with consulting assignments and one-time payments.)

The entrepreneur's motivation may be a key to the actual arrangement. The entrepreneur should do what he does well and what he likes to do. For example, many entrepreneurs assume they will want to sell their own product. The hard fact of life is that not all people are good salespeople and even fewer enjoy it. In the case of sales aversion, the entrepreneur may be highly motivated to turn the product over to a larger firm. Most entrepreneurs are highly motivated from a monetary standpoint. If they are realistic, they realize that 20 percent of $1 million in revenue without personal discomfort and expense is much better than $200,000 earned with much frustration and personal liability. Again the key is to do what you really want to do. Many people simply do not enjoy running a large company. These motivational factors assist the large company in working with software entrepreneurs.

The iceberg phenomenon is foreign to many software entrepreneurs. There is an enormous amount of work beyond the coding effort. The work involved in marketing, documentation, brochures, slides, competitive analysis, sales kits, product distribution, quality assurance, and support often exceeds the coding effort by a factor of five. The investment in this additional effort is substantial, and large software firms are prepared to invest the necessary funds.

Most large software firms are very concerned with sales and marketing. They realize that good products are essential but that a major key to growth is a working sales and marketing organization. The investment in building a sales force is substantial. A large company views a new salesperson via this simple model: If the person can sell and has experience, and if he knows the territory, he can become productive in three to five months after at least a month of training. This is a long-term investment in productivity. The general rule is that an average salesperson produces $350,000 per year in revenue. However, at least one out of four new hires are complete failures. The better firms recognize this and avoid hiring new individuals who are bad risks. In this case, Mr. Coleman's quote is, "Bad breath is *not* better than no breath." Too much energy is wasted on poor salespeople. Why is this important to the software entrepreneur? The sales force is a valuable asset to a large company and it does not react to change quickly. The same type of training required for a new member of the sales force is required for a new product. The entrepreneur must recognize that although the company's success might be at the $700,000 per year level, the large sales force will produce fewer sales per person. Of course, a key to this is the investment in the sales force and the benefit that it can bring to the entrepreneur.

Finally, a large software firm is very aware of its distribution channels and the economics of these channels. For example, if the product is suitable for telephone sales or mail order sales, the large firm can often pass on additional royalty percentages. If the product has a great deal of international appeal, a nondomestic sales force is very important. In general, the entrepreneur faces a very difficult task in finding international outlets. Most large firms have already established these channels. The better the fit with the firm's channels, the more attractive the deal.

With those factors in mind, the biggest stumbling block to an attractive deal is the unrealistic view of the product author who believes that the product has an unlimited potential. (Author's note: One additional stumbling block is that the large company may be so "thorough" or so slow in its evaluation process that the software entrepreneur is completely alienated by the process. Unfortunately, only a few large companies are geared to perform this type of evaluation in a professional manner.)

The best way for a software entrepreneur to deal with the larger companies is to assemble outside help. There are recognized individuals who have structured these types of arrangements. They can objectively assist the developer in the negotiating process. There are also attorneys and accountants who have put together the contracts associated with software procurement. They are able to protect the interests of the entrepreneur without requiring a great deal of education as to what the arrangement will look like. Mr. Coleman recommends that if you do not know of such outside advisors, you should check with others who have been there. They can recommend individuals. Even so, check references. Most large software firms would prefer to work with an entrepreneur who has such advisors since the effort will be more productive.

The preferred deal is one whereby the company achieves ownership of the product and the author has both up-front dollars and a royalty stream. Usually the firm wishes some assistance from key people. This means that the entrepreneur can provide maintenance and assistance in other areas while the large firm gears up. This close relationship usually lasts a year or so. In most cases, a full-time product manager launches the product and a "tiger team" takes over the technical efforts, including quality assurance. It is an excellent idea to have a very early product walkthrough so that the final effort will be based on knowledge rather than chance.

There will be obvious conflicts between the entrepreneur and the acquiring company. Usually the author believes that he or she knows how to sell the system and dislikes the company's methods. This knowledge is useful and can assist the larger firm if it does not get in the way of the actual effort. Technically, all products can be improved, and it is best to try to work together to improve the system. The developer/entrepreneur should be sensitive to the fact that key technical employees of the large firm have some resentment of outside products since they would prefer to develop systems. Maturity and teamwork overcome this.

As a final note, there are certain valid reasons for not dealing with a large firm. The entrepreneur might be able to make more money on his own. There are many very successful small companies. Additionally, the entrepreneur may not wish to give up control and should not be coerced into this if it is a major factor. In some cases, entrepreneurs like to build an organization and enjoy the effort. In such cases, the entrepreneur might be happier and more successful not dealing with a large software firm.

INDEX